Patience is a priceless gem.
But few know how it's mined.
If we can learn to use it well,
Everything will turn out fine.
--Master Hua

Without a doubt, the greatest strength the Master provided was his personal presence day in and day out, year in and year out, as he nurtured the seeds and tended the sprouts of Buddhism in the West.

The Master came to the West to plant good seeds
in the hearts and minds of Westerners. He vowed to
establish a traditional Sangha order of fully-ordained
monks and nuns; to oversee the translation and
dissemination of the Buddhists scriptures and texts;
to set up institutes of learning that placed
emphasis on providing students
with solid moral foundations upon
which they could go on to better
serve humankind.

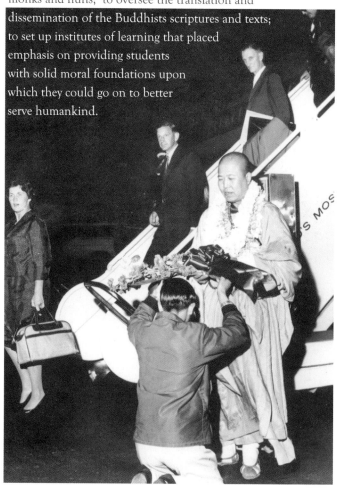

The Venerable Master with  his first five American monastic disciples.

Let me tell you what my work is: it's coarse work; I'm a brick maker. Bricks must be fired so they don't crumble. For a year the five of you have been fired and fired and now the time is ripe. You are like bricks that have been sufficiently fired and can be used to build a Dharma house that will have a firm foundation.

Master Hua, October 29, 1969

Master Hua shows disciples the sharira of Elder Master Hsu Yun.

Five-colored in profusion are the solid seeds;
Perfectly forged, the myriad virtues, like the full moon.

Disciple Hsuan Hua in Praise of Master Yun's sharira

Master and disciples circumambulate on the roof of the Buddhist Lecture Hall, Chinatown, San Francisco, 1970.

"Once we form a circle, then the positions of first and last lose their meaning. Last becomes first; first becomes last. Everyone can be first; everyone can be last," The Master pointed out. He used the circle as an analogy in teaching disciples about fighting, competition, ambition, and greed for fame and position.

4

The Master's wise and gentle kindness was a compelling force that attracted beings of all kinds. Here, the lessons this bird learned about greed for food were not lost on the Master's human disciples who observed these non-verbal teachings.

Lessons in Sanskrit, Japanese, French, German, Portuguese, Spanish, Chinese, and Pali were a vital part of the education that took place at Gold Mountain Dhyana Monastery. Here, David Rounds teaches English composition.

In the early '70's, the Master and members of the Buddhist Text Translation Society joined a workshop in Stonybrook, New York that explored the beginnings of a multi-lingual Buddhist dictionary project.

The Buddhist Text Translation Society, founded in 1970, established a four-part process for the translation of each title: primary translation, review of translation, editing of translation, certification of translation.

A group portrait at Gold Mountain Dhyana Monastery. Several of these children later became some of the first students of Instilling Goodness Elementary School, founded by the Master.

The Master directs a passing of offerings ceremony- the first time it was performed at Gold Mountain Monastery.

The Master kept a low profile and encouraged his monastic disciples to take the lead and learn through direct experience.

Disciple: What does community work involve?

Master: We must not be lazy when it comes to community work, which includes attending morning and evening services in the Buddha Hall like everyone else. Follow the norms that the community has established for rising and sleeping, moving and resting. Those who try to act differently than others in a monastery are prohibited from living with the group. People should not try to be unique in a monastic setting. On top of that, they have to be most respectful and earnest if they are to realize right enlightenment.

The Master hosted a Dharma Gathering to Liberate the Living
at Berkeley Marina in 1974 on the anniversary of the enlightenment of
Guan Yin Bodhisattva.
By liberating creatures whose lives are doomed, we can liberate ourselves
and the world from the effects that killing karma brings about.

During a retreat at Buddha Root Farm
in Oregon, the Master taught Westerns
about Amitabha Buddha's vows to help
those who recite his name to gain rebirth
in the Western Pure Land. Participants
chanted and meditated in a tent during
the week-long session.
On the final evening, everyone went to the
coast and performed the Great Transference
of Merit as the sun set in the west.

Master with disciples who undertook a pilgrimage for the sake of world peace by bowing once every three steps from San Francisco to Marblemount, Washington.

The Master's sense of humor was a compelling attraction for many Westerners. The monk Heng Ju especially enjoyed it and loved to tell stories to illustrate the Master's wit. The "pie" story is a classic. Wait for it in this series!

The Master greets Heng Sure upon his arrival at the City of Ten Thousand Buddhas at the culmination a bowing pilgrimage once every three steps from Los Angeles. The records of that pilgrimage fill volumes. In this volume see "A Good and Wise Advisor's Teachings for Me."

In the early '70's sincere lay people from Los Angeles requested the Master and disciples to travel there and perform a Taking Refuge Ceremony, so that they could formally become Buddhists. Gold Wheel Monastery was founded shortly after this visit and the Dharma began to spread in Southern California.

Good and wise advisors,
take refuge with the Triple Jewel
of your own nature:
The Buddha, which is awakening;
The Dharma, which is right;
The Sangha, which is pure.
Our own mind takes refuge
with awakening, the honored
complete in blessings and wisdom.
Our own mind takes refuge
with what is right,
the honored apart from desire.

Let us wash clean the body and mind; brush away accumulated dirt; develop a sense of shame; change our past faults; become unique and awesome people full of vitality; do beneficial deeds for the sake of all beings; and create virtue on behalf of all humankind.

Excerpt from Tomorrow, an essay by Master Hua

How
Buddhism
Changed
My
Life!

The Moon Reflected in a Thousand Rivers

Stories of Master Hsuan Hua
by his disciples

How
Buddhism
Changed
My
Life!

Buddhist Text Translation Society
Dharma Realm Buddhist University
Dharma Realm Buddhist Association

Buddhist Text Translation Society
1777 Murchison Drive,
Burlingame, CA 94010-4504

The Moon Reflected in a Thousand Rivers

Stories of Master Hsuan Hua told by his disciples

Series: ISBN 0-88139-490-4

Published by: Buddhist Text Translation Society
Dharma Realm Buddhist University
Dharma Realm Buddhist Association

http://www.drba.org
http://www.bttsonline.org

How Buddhism Changed My Life - Vol. 1

Published by:

Buddhist Text Translation Society
1777 Murchison Drive, Burlingame,
CA 94010-4504

@ 2003 Buddhist Text Translation Society
Dharma Realm Buddhist Association
Dharma Realm Buddhist University

Printed in Taiwan

First Edition 2003

10 09 08 07 06 05 04 03   1 2 3 4 5 6 7 8

Library of Congress Cataloging-in-Publication Data

How my entire life was changed! / Compiled by the Buddhist Text
Translation Society.— 1st ed.
p. cm. — (Master Hsèuan Hua. Teaching and transforming ; vol.1)

ISBN 0-88139-487-4
1. Hsèuan Hua, 1908- I. Buddhist Text Translation Society. II. Series.

BQ962.S767 H68 2003
294.3'92'092—dc21

2002012675

CONTENTS

APPENDIX:

PREFACE:

A MAGNIFICENT LIVING EXAMPLE OF THE DHARMA

—I just want to express the gratitude from the Western side of Buddhism to the Great Master, who inspired us all and gave us so much during his lifetime. It's a great gift from the Asian continent to the Western world, these venerable sages that choose to live and share their wisdom with us in the Western world. I think this kind of gift and great compassion is something beyond compare. It is what you might call "foreign aid at its very best." I will always remember and treasure this.

Also, in reflecting on the body of the great Master this morning, I had a marvelous insight into the way he would say he was always living like a dead man anyway. The truth, the pure Dharma, that which is real and true, was never born and never dies. Even though the Great Master, in terms of conventions of our language and our perceptual range, is such that we see Venerable Master Hua as having died and passed away, what we really loved and respected is still present with us, and that is the True Dharma that he was always pointing to and of which he was a magnificent living example. I just want to say again what gratitude we all feel—here in America and Europe—for the great gifts that the Venerable Master gave to us.

EVERYTHING HE DID WAS TO BENEFIT OTHERS AND NEVER FOR HIMSELF

—In retrospect, the vigor, depth and breadth of the Master's efforts in teaching in the West are nothing short of incredible. In his early days of teaching Westerners, he often had little or no help. He cooked, taught them to cook, sat with them in meditation and taught them to sit, entertained them with Buddhist stories, and taught them the rudiments of Buddhadharma and Buddhist courtesy and ceremony. He gave lessons in Chinese and in Chinese calligraphy, and taught the fundamentals of the pure Buddhist lifestyle.

Much of the Master's most important teaching took place outside of his formal Dharma lectures. For the Master, every situation was an opportunity for teaching, and he paid little attention to whether the recipients of instruction were formal disciples. For him every worldly encounter, whether with disciples or politicians or realtors, was an opportunity to help people become aware of their faults and change them and to develop their inherent wisdom. The Master was open, direct, and totally honest with everyone in every situation. He treated everyone equally, from the President of the United States to little children. Everything he did was to benefit others and never for himself.

—Perhaps most valuable to me is that the Master gave ultimate meaning to my life. He showed me every day in his every single action that the wonderful world of the Buddha-dharma portrayed in the Sutras is not fantasy, fairy tale or intellectual abstraction. He showed me that it is real and alive, and even more importantly, a possibility and practical ideal for our own lives. I remember him saying that we should explain the Sutras as if we ourselves had spoken them, to make them our own and not distance ourselves from them. Clearly that is the example that he expressed through his own life.

EDITORIAL NOTE:

The Youth Good Wealth contemplated and reflected upon the instructions of his Good and Wise Advisor: He was like the great sea, which receives the rains from the great clouds without satiation. He had the following thought:

The Good and Wise Advisor's teaching is like a spring sun in that it produces and makes grow the roots and sprouts of all good Dharmas;

The Good and Wise Advisor's teaching is like a full moon, in that it refreshes and cools everything it shines on;

The Good and Wise Advisor's teaching is like a snow mountain in summer, in that it can dispel the heat and thirst of all beasts;

The Good and Wise Advisor's teaching is like the sun on a fragrant pool, in that it can open the lotus flower of the mind of all goodness;

The Good and Wise Advisor's teaching is like a great jeweled continent, in that the various Dharma jewels fill his heart;

The Good and Wise Advisor's teaching is like the Jambu tree, in that it amasses the flowers and fruits of all blessings and wisdom;

The Good and Wise Advisor's teaching is like a great dragon king, in that he playfully roams with ease and comfort in empty space;

The Good and Wise Advisor's teaching is like Mt. Sumeru, in that limitless wholesome dharmas of the Heaven of the Thirty-three are situated in its midst;

The Good and Wise Advisor's teaching is like Lord Shakra, who is circumambulated by his multitudes and assemblies, in that none can overshadow him, and who can subdue bizarre cults and hosts of Asura armies. In this way he reflected — the *Avatamsaka Sutra*

More than 3000 years ago, when Confucius taught, by far the most outstanding aspect of his teaching was his policy of accepting anyone who wanted to learn, regardless of their status in society. That is why, despite the turmoil of the times, 3000 disciples studied with him. In these contemporary times, not only did the Venerable Master Hua teach anyone who wanted to learn, he taught each individual using methods appropriate to him or her, and never renounced a single living being. Despite the chaos that now prevails, hundreds of thousands drew near the Master to learn from him. In this book there are some accounts of things that happened as the Master teaching his disciples.

BIOGRAPHICAL SKETCH OF THE VENERABLE MASTER HSUAN HUA

The Venerable Master, a native of Shuangcheng County of Jilin Province, was born on the sixteenth day of the third lunar month in the year of Wu. Wu at the beginning of the century. His family surname was Bai and his name was Yushu. He was also called Yuxi. His father, Bai Fuhai, was diligent and thrifty in managing the household. His mother, whose maiden name was Hu, ate only vegetarian food and recited the Buddha's name every day throughout her life. When she was pregnant with the Master, she prayed to the Buddhas and Bodhisattvas. The night before his birth, in a dream she saw Amitabha Buddha emitting brilliant light. Following that the Master was born.

As a child, the Master followed his mother's example and ate only vegetarian food and recited the Buddha's name. The Master was quiet and untalkative by nature, but he had a righteous and heroic spirit. At the age of eleven, upon seeing a neighbor's infant who had died, he became aware of the great matter of birth and death and the brevity of life and resolved to leave the home-life. At the age of twelve, he heard of how Filial Son Wong of Shuangcheng County (later known as Great Master Chang Ren) had practiced filial piety and attained the Way, and he vowed to follow the Filial Son's example. Repenting for being unfilial to his parents in the past, the Master decided to bow to his parents every morning and evening as a way of acknowledging his faults and repaying his parents' kindness. He gradually became renowned for his filial conduct, and people called him Filial Son Bai. At fifteen, he took refuge under the Venerable Master Chang Zhi. That same year he began to attend school and mastered the Four Books, the Five Classics, the texts of various Chinese schools of thought, and the fields of medicine, divination, astrology, and physiognomy. During his student years, he also participated in the Moral Society and other charitable societies. He explained the *Sixth Patriarch's Sutra*, the *Vajra Sutra*, and other Sutras for those who were illiterate, and started a free school for those who were poor and needy. When he was nineteen, his mother passed away, and he requested Venerable Master Chang Zhi of Sanyuan (Three Conditions) Monastery to shave his head. He was given the Dharma name An Tse and style name To Lun. Dressed in the left-home robes, he built a simple hut by his mother's grave and observed the practice of filial piety. During that period, he made eighteen great vows, bowed to the *Avatamsaka (Flower Adornment) Sutra*, performed worship and pure repentance, practiced Chan meditation, studied the teachings, ate only one meal a day, and did not lie down to sleep at night. As his skill grew ever more pure, he won the admiration and respect of the villagers. His intensely sincere efforts to purify and cultivate himself moved the Buddhas and Bodhisattvas as well as the Dharma-protecting gods and dragons. The miraculous responses were too many to be counted. As news of these supernatural events spread far and wide, the Master came to be regarded as an extraordinary monk. One day as he was sitting in meditation, he saw the Great Master, the Sixth Patriarch, come to his hut and tell him, "In the future you will go to the West, where you will meet limitless and boundless numbers of people. The living beings you teach and transform will be as countless as the sands of the Ganges River. That will mark the beginning of the Buddhadharma in the West."

After the Sixth Patriarch finished speaking, he suddenly vanished. When his observance of filial piety was completed, the Master went to Changbai Mountain and dwelled in seclusion in the Amitabha Cave, where he practiced austerities. Later he returned to Sanyuan Monastery, where he was chosen to be the head of the assembly. During the period that he lived in Manchuria, the Master contemplated people's potentials and bestowed appropriate teachings. He awakened those who were confused and saved many people's lives. Countless dragons, snakes, foxes, ghosts, and spirits requested to take refuge and receive the precepts from him, changing their evil and cultivating goodness.

In 1946, because he esteemed the Elder Master Hsu Yun as a great hero of Buddhism, the Master quickly packed his belongings and set out on his way to pay homage to him. During his arduous journey, he stayed at many of the renowned monasteries of mainland China. In 1947 he went to Potola Mountain to receive the complete ordination. In 1948 he reached Nanhua Monastery at Caoxi of Guangzhou, where he paid homage to Elder Master Hsu Yun and was assigned to be an instructor in the Nanhua Monastery Vinaya Academy. Later he was appointed as Dean of Academic Affairs. The Elder Master Hsu Yun saw that the Master was an outstanding individual in Buddhism and transmitted the Dharma-lineage to him, giving him the Dharma name Hsuan Hua and making him the Ninth Patriarch of the Wei Yang Sect, the forty-fifth generation since the First Patriarch Mahakashyapa.

In 1949, the Master bid farewell to the Venerable Master Hsu Yun and went to Hong Kong to propagate the Dharma. He gave equal importance to the five schools—Chan, Doctrine, Vinaya, Esoteric, and Pure Land—thus putting an end to sectarianism. The Master also renovated old temples, printed Sutras and constructed images. He established Western Bliss Gardens Monastery, Cixing Chan Monastery, and the Buddhist Lecture Hall. He lived in Hong Kong for more than ten years, and at the earnest request of living beings, he created extensive affinities in the Dharma. He delivered a succession of lectures on the *Earth Store Sutra*, the *Vajra Sutra*, the *Amitabha Sutra*, the *Shurangama Sutra*, the Universal Door Chapter, and others. In addition, he held various Dharma assemblies such as the Great Compassion Repentance, the Medicine Master Repentance, recitation sessions, and meditation sessions. He also published the magazine *Hsin Fa (Mind Dharma)*. Every day he worked and travelled zealously for the sake of propagating the great Dharma, and as a result the Buddhadharma flourished in Hong Kong. During that time he also made several visits to Thailand, Burma, and other countries to investigate the southern (Theravada) tradition of Buddhism. He wished to establish communication between the Mahayana and Theravada traditions and unite the strength of Buddhism.

In 1959, the Master saw that conditions were ripe in the West, and he instructed his disciples to establish the Sino-American Buddhist Association (later renamed the Dharma Realm Buddhist Association) in the United States. He travelled to Australia in 1961 and propagated the Dharma there for one year. Since the conditions were not yet ripe there, he returned to Hong Kong in 1962. That same year, at the invitation of Buddhists in America, the Master traveled alone to the United States. He raised the banner of proper Dharma at the Buddhist Lecture Hall in San Francisco. Because the Master started out living in a damp and windowless basement that resembled a grave, he called himself "The Monk in the Grave." At that time the Cuban missile crisis occurred between the United States and the Soviet Union, and the Master embarked on a total fast for thirty-five days to pray for an end to the hostilities and for world peace. By the end of his fast, the threat of war had dissolved.

In 1968, the Shurangama Study and Practice Summer Session was held, and over thirty students from the University of Washington in Seattle came to study the Buddhadharma. After the session was concluded, five young Americans requested permission to shave their heads and leave the home-life, marking the beginning of the Sangha in the history of American Buddhism. Since that time, the Venerable Master devoted his utmost efforts to such tasks as propagating the Dharma, supervising the translation of the Buddhist Canon, and developing education. He accepted vast numbers of disciples, established monasteries, and set forth principles. He focused the earnest sincerity of all disciples on the work of glorifying the Proper Dharma of the Thus Come One to the ends of time and throughout empty space and the Dharma Realm.

In terms of propagating the Dharma, the Master lectured on the Sutras and expounded the Dharma virtually every single day for several decades, always giving simple explanations that made profound principles easy to understand. He also worked actively to train both his left-home and lay disciples to become skilled in propagating the Dharma. He led many delegations to propagate the Dharma at various universities and in many countries of the world, with the goal of guiding living beings to reform and to discover their innate wisdom.

As for the translation of the Buddhist Canon, to date over a hundred volumes of the Master's explanations of the scriptures have been translated into English. No one else has overseen the translation of so many Sutras into English. Translations into Spanish, Vietnamese, and other languages have also been produced. His plans were to translate the entire Buddhist Canon into the languages of every country, so that the Buddhadharma could spread throughout the world.

As for education, at the City of Ten Thousand Buddhas he established such educational institutions as Instilling Goodness Elementary School, Developing Virtue Secondary School, Dharma Realm Buddhist University, and the Sangha and Laity Training Programs. Many of the affiliated monasteries also have weekend and weekday classes based on the eight fundamental human virtues of filiality, fraternal respect, loyalty, trustworthiness, propriety, righteousness, incorruptibility, and a sense of shame. Taking the public-spirited, unselfish spirit of kindness, compassion, joy, and giving as their goal, boys and girls study separately and the volunteer teachers regard education as their personal responsibility. In this way, students develop into capable individuals of incorruptible integrity who will be able to save the world.

The Master taught his disciples that every day they should sit in meditation, recite the Buddha's name, bow in repentance, investigate the Sutras, rigorously uphold the precepts, eat only one meal a day, and only before noon, and always wear the precept sash. He instructed them to dwell in harmony and offer encouragement to each other. In this way he established a Sangha that genuinely practices the Buddhadharma in the West, in the hope of uplifting the orthodox teaching and causing the Proper Dharma to long abide. The Venerable Master also opened up the City of Ten Thousand Buddhas as an international religious center promoting the unity of all world religions by giving everyone a chance to learn, communicate, cooperate, pursue the truth, and work for world peace.

Throughout his life the Venerable Master was totally selfless. He vowed to take the suffering and hardships of all living beings upon himself, and to dedicate all his own blessings and joy to the living beings of the Dharma Realm. He practiced what was difficult to practice and endured what was difficult to endure, persevering in his heroic and pure resolve. He was a candle that refused to be blown out by the gale, an irreducible lump of pure gold in the hot fire. The Venerable Master composed a verse expressing his principles:

Freezing to death, we do not scheme.
Starving to death, we do not beg.
Dying of poverty, we ask for nothing.
According with conditions, we do not change.
Not changing, we accord with conditions.
We adhere firmly to our three great principles.

We renounce our lives to do the Buddha's work.
We take the responsibility to mold our own destinies.
We rectify our lives as the Sangha's work.
Encountering specific matters, we understand the principles.
Understanding the principles, we apply them in specific matters.
We carry on the single pulse of the patriarchs' mind-transmission.

From the time he left the home-life, the Venerable Master firmly maintained the six great principles—do not fight, do not be greedy, do not seek, do not be selfish, do not pursue personal advantage, and do not lie—bringing benefit to the multitudes. Teaching with wisdom and compassion, dedicating himself to serving others, and acting as a model for others, he influenced countless people to sincerely change their faults and head towards the pure and exalted Bodhi Way.

Living beings of the present have deep obstructions and scarce blessings indeed, for a Sage of the era has abruptly manifested passing into stillness. The living beings of the Saha world have suddenly lost their harbor of refuge. Yet the life of the Venerable Master is actually an enactment of the great *Flower Adornment Sutra* of the Dharma Realm. Although he has manifested entry into Nirvana, he constantly turns the infinite wheel—not leaving any traces, he came from empty space, and to empty space he returned. His disciples can only carefully follow their teacher's instructions, hold fast to their principles, honor the Buddha's regulations, and be ever more vigorous in advancing upon the path to Bodhi so that they can repay the Venerable Master's boundless and profound grace.

The truth, the pure Dharma, that which is our real nature,
was never born and never dies. Even though the Great Master,
in terms of the conventions of our language and our perceptual
range, is such that we see Venerable Master Hsuan Hua as having
died and passed away, what we really loved and respected is still
present with us: the true Dharma that he was always pointing
to and of which he was a magnificent living example.

LIFE
WITH
THE
MASTER

ര   Richard Josephson
(Guo Hang)

When I arrived back in the U.S. from India, I went to the San Francisco Zen Center to practice Buddhism. But, after only a week I became discouraged because I was used to a much more vigorous practice. One of the people there told me of Gold Mountain. He said that few people go there because the practice is so difficult. I went to Gold Mountain the following day, and the first thing I saw on the wall was a picture of the Master Hsu Yun. I enquired about the picture and a monk there told me that Master Hua carried his lineage, but unfortunately the Master was on a South American tour and would not return for two months. I said that this was no obstacle, and I waited in the Buddha Hall for two months, sleeping under the stairs.

My practice during my earlier years at Gold Mountain was the recitation of mantras and cleaning the temple, and this is what it remained for the entire ten years I was with the Master.

It is difficult to relate a sudden awakening or a sudden non-awakening to another because the interaction between a ripe student and his teacher (or circumstance) is a very personal one. For example, Master Hsu Yun had a major awakening when hot tea was accidentally poured on his hand. The cultivation that ripened Master Hsu Yun's mind for his awakening took

1

many months and his state of mind at that moment was unique to Master Hsu Yun. If this were not the case, anyone who had hot tea poured on his hand could obtain enlightenment. Having no sudden awakening to share, I would like to share a sudden non-awakening. As painful as non-awakenings were they too formed an important part of my cultivation.

I once handed the Master a gatha that read: "To see Amitabha in the Western Pure Land; how can this be done when facing East?" At that time, I was in charge of the meditation hall at Gold Mountain and always faced East during my many hours of daily meditation. The question put to the Master was from my heart and not merely a Zen game. In order to appreciate the Master's reply, one has to know something of the Master's third floor room at Gold Mountain. The walls and ceiling were supported by offerings from lay people, which included thousands of bars of soap and toothbrushes, piled everywhere with no order whatsoever. When one visited the Master's room he would often stick his hand in one of the piles and give you something. The Master couldn't read the English labeling, and never looked anyway, but nevertheless it often seemed as if the Master gave you just what you needed.

For the weeks that followed my giving the Master my gatha, I continued my meditations awaiting the Master's reply. Unfortunately I didn't recognize it when it came unexpectedly one day as I sat meditating alone in the Buddhahall. The Master used to be able to break my meditation by looking at me. As I meditated in the hall he caused me to be aware of his presence on the far side of the hall near the office. He began walking towards me. He looked very different. He was expressionless, deep in trance, and not looking at me. But as he passed my bench he gave me a toothbrush. Then he continued on to circumambulate the Buddha, still deep in trance, in reverse direction, with the Buddha on his left. Only Shr Fu and myself were in the Buddhahall. I looked a moment at the toothbrush, saw nothing peculiar about it, and put it under my meditation bench. Shr Fu continued around the Buddha in reverse circumambulation.

A week passed before I thought to have another look at the toothbrush. I then realized, with my heart in my stomach, the brand name of the toothbrush: Dr. West.

One of the Master's most important teachings was that a disciple should not attach to "marks" or the form of a practice. Shr Fu helped us to realize a lofty purpose in our practice. When Heng Ju left to bow over a thousand miles to see his mother he failed after a single day. He didn't have the right motivation to sustain his pilgrimage. However, after he returned defeated to Gold Mountain, the Master gently directed Heng Ju's viewpoint from a purely selfish and egotistic one, to a lofty and altruistic one—World Peace. After that, Heng Ju completed his bows from San Francisco to Marblemount, Washington.

Now that Shr Fu is no longer with us, it is our duty as his disciples to make sure that Shr Fu does not become a mere memory. I personally feel a deeper sense of urgency to spread Buddhism now that Shr Fu is gone than I did when the Master was still with us. Shr Fu has carried his torch (his body) for as long as he could, doing the work of a Bodhisattva. Now he has passed the torch on to all of us. It is not only our duty as disciples to carry on the Master's work, but also the best way we can honor our Teacher.

Every day do something in honor of the Master and allow that seed to sprout. Shr Fu taught Dharma to all of us who have been touched by him. That very special feeling that each of us feels in his heart for the Master is his Dharma transmission. Without trying to intellectualize it, allow it to work through you.

If someone were to ask me what is the most important thing I gained from being with the Master for ten years, I would have to say that it is my deep conviction that I am Buddhist and my faith in the Buddhist teachings. When I first entered Gold Mountain, the idea of obtaining enlightenment seemed very remote and impossible. I was more concerned with ending this life's afflictions. But, after years with the Master my aim changed. I now understand that one must resolve to cultivate to end birth and death and realize the Bodhisattva ideal. Shr Fu pushed us all to "do what others cannot do," so that we might have an experiential awareness of the truth of Buddhism rather than a merely intellectual one. Woven within all my daily thoughts is a Buddhist thread, a thread that holds the fabric of my being together, and Shr Fu within my heart. The conviction that I am a Buddhist is unshakable.

A TEACHING
BY THE
VENERABLE
MASTER

ଔ Shr Heng Hsien

When I first left home I was very arrogant about my ability to stay awake when meditating while others fell asleep. Then my retribution came, and I got so that I fell asleep as soon as I sat down. It became a big problem. In those days, we could ask the Venerable Master about all sorts of things, and because I was very concerned about my sleeping problem, I pleaded with the Venerable Master to help me with it. Of course, skill in meditation is something one has to develop oneself, and there are no magic formulas to make things easy. However, the Venerable Master employed an unusual method to aid me. It was the L.A. bus.

I had become so desperate to find some way out of my dilemma that I had even made a vow before the great assembly that I would not fall asleep during meditation. Right away a fellow-cultivator planted a doubt in my mind by saying to me and others that I should not have made a vow I could not keep. And I didn't manage to keep the vow. Because I didn't keep it, many things in my life and cultivation started to go wrong. It's hard to interpret what that means when such things happen. One starts to doubt in various ways when right in the midst of such states; but in retrospect they might just be part of a change that will lead in time to progress out of a difficult impasse.

In any case, my turn came to be sent to Los Angeles. In those days, the nuns used to take turns going to live in Gold Wheel Temple in Los Angeles. The Venerable Master went to L.A. every month, and that's when we would go down or come back. Fortunately, the month I went down it was not by car. That month our big bus drove there, and a lot of people went. I believe it was in the early 1980's, although without research I don't know the exact date; and we were staying at the third Gold Wheel which was on 6th Street in downtown L.A. When my turn was completed, I was also fortunate. I say fortunate, because I always carry a lot of things with me when I travel, so I also needed to take many things back with me. But the bus had come down again, so I thought there would be no problem.

However, on Monday morning when it was time to board the bus, the Venerable Master unexpectedly announced, in a loud and displeased voice for all to hear, that I was not allowed to get on the bus. His reason? He told me and all the people who had come to see him off, along with all the people who were going back on the bus, that the bus was not for someone as lazy as I who fell asleep as soon as she sat down! With that, the bus drove away without me, and I was left very astonished and remorseful in L.A.

Actually, it was a beautiful, sunny morning in Los Angeles, and Gold Wheel Temple was filled with joyous light and wholesome energy from the Venerable Master's visit. But I just felt deeply ashamed and repentant. I didn't even try to think of what to do. I just went into what had been my room for the past month and meditated. You can imagine I didn't fall asleep that time! I just reviewed my spinelessness and lack of resolve, and was profoundly sorry. Then after about half an hour we heard noise in the parking lot. The bus had returned and I was allowed to get on it after all! Other nuns told me later that the bus had driven off, and after awhile on the highway the Venerable Master had told the driver to turn around and go back to Gold Wheel—to get me.

I think it's hard for people who did not experience it to realize the amount of energy and resourcefulness the Venerable Master put into teaching his disciples. When I received that teaching, I was, as with many similar teachings, intensely focused on the immediate situation. But looking back I can see the Venerable Master's incredible compassion and how much he helped me get through a very difficult period—by having a bus travel so far with all those people and then come back, pushing me to the brink of remorse, and then giving me the joy of being forgiven and the underlying assurance that the Venerable Master cared that much about whether I cultivated or not. He had responded to my repeated pleas for help in a most dramatic way, with a lesson that went very deep. How much others might have learned from it as well is also hard to estimate, but certainly that, too, must have been part of the teaching.

I'm slow, and it will probably be a long time before I never fall asleep in meditation. But I did improve after that amazing teaching. And remembering it now, I feel that there must have been something planted by it which may take a lot of time to grow, but which eventually will lead to a kind of strength to fulfill an "impossible" vow—not with arrogance but with humility and gratitude.

TRY
YOUR
BEST!

ଓଃ Helen Woo

In the early years when I was with the Master, many Americans and people who did not speak Chinese wanted to draw near the Master, so I would translate for them. At the closing of meetings, the Master would always say in English, "Try your best!" I bear these few words in mind as if they are seals, deeply ingrained in the bottom of my heart. Whatever I do, I always remember these words, "Try your best!" They provide a very helpful strength. They encourage me when I encounter adverse states. They are a tool which has helped me in changing from bad to wholesome, and thus enabled me to become a truly useful person in this life.

Before I met the Master, the kind of life I lived made me feel that I was useless to this society. I was very naughty, and only knew how to enjoy myself. I came to the United States when I was only fifteen, and therefore was not steeped in traditional Chinese culture for very long. I got married right after college graduation. My husband's income as a physician is more than adequate to support the family. So I spent my time indulging in pleasure: dancing, singing, performing amateur Chinese opera, playing cards, and drinking. I did everything and lived a life in which day and night were turned upside-down. In general, my life was quite meaningless, and I didn't do any work except for raising two children.

After my father passed away in 1969, I started thinking, "He couldn't have disappeared just because his flesh body is gone. Where did his soul go?" I wanted to know why I came to this world, and where I will be going in the future. I had many questions of this sort which I knew Christianity could not answer. I began searching for answers. It occurred to me that perhaps Buddhism could answer my questions. Buddhism must have some profound principles. However, at that time (around 1970), there was no Buddhist temple in southern California, and I did not know any Buddhists. Buddhism simply did not exist in my life. It was under these circumstances that I started my search for the true principles of Buddhism. When I first heard the principles of Buddhism, I was overjoyed. So the Buddhadharma was this great! So every one of us could become a Buddha! This is great! So all of us were of one substance, and the myriad things were originally of the same substance! It was only because of our ignorance, plus the three poisons of greed, anger and stupidity, that we have been transmigrating back and forth in the six paths, undergoing all kinds of suffering.

I knew then that I wanted to have a teacher of proper Dharma. Since I didn't know the Master was in San Francisco, I went to Taiwan with some friends to take refuge with Dharma Master Guang Qin in 1976. After I returned to the States, I realized that, "Things which are thought to be as far away as the horizon, are actually right in front of your eyes." Through friends, I came to know the Master, an eminent monk right in the city of San Francisco. I was really lucky; this must have been due to some wholesome roots that I had planted in my past lives.

We decided to hurry up and take refuge with the Master. After discussing it with friends, the number of people who wanted to take refuge increased to over ten. We had planned to take the plane, but seeing the growing number of people, we rented a bus instead. That was still not enough, for the number of people continued to increase. What were we to do? We didn't know the Master personally, so we went to the friend who had introduced the Master to us. Since we were taking refuge, we really should have gone to the Master's place; how could we ask the Master to come to us? But because there were too many people, we were forced to make the request, which the Master very compassionately granted. I immediately went to rent the big South Pasadena Modonic Hall, and made a huge sign to welcome the Master and his disciples at the airport. The Master took this matter very seriously and brought many disciples with him. He also brought over many sutras, both in Chinese and English. I had never met the Master or organized any Buddhist event before this. Although this was the first time, we still had to do it well.

The refuge ceremony was solemn. The eldest participant was over eighty years old, and the youngest was a baby. It went perfectly. Since I was very busy that day, I didn't have a chance to take a good look at the Master. The next morning when I got up, the Master was sitting in my living room. I walked over and knelt before him, and then I took a good look at him. All of a sudden, I broke down. From the bottom of my heart I felt this bitter sensation, and started crying out aloud, "Waaa......" My feelings were a mixture of a myriad kinds of pain and joy. It was hard to describe. Sorrow and joy co-mingled.

I cried for a long, long time. The Master said to me in a very kind and compassionate way, "Now you have come home." Then he asked me, "What is your maiden name?" I said, "Yu." He said, "Where were you originally from?" I said, "San Francisco." "What was your father's name?" I told him. Ah! My father and the Master were good friends! Since my father was very interested in Chinese culture, after the Master came to the States, the two had become good friends. However, since I had already married and moved to Los Angeles, the conditions were not ripe for me to meet the Master. In fact, my father had known the Master since 1962, and I had to wait until after my father passed away (1976) to meet the Master and take refuge with him.

After we took refuge, the Master transmitted the five precepts to us. I smoked and drank then. The Master said: "After you have taken refuge, you should not smoke again. The Bodhisattvas do not like people to smoke. If you smoke, the smell of it will drive the Bodhisattvas away." So I quit smoking. Not smoking was not a big problem for me because I never liked smoking. I just joined in with friends when we were playing mahjong. However, to quit drinking was very difficult for me because I had loved to drink ever since I was young. My husband always worried that I would become an alcoholic one day. So I always tell him, "You should be thankful and filial to the Master, because he has saved both your life and mine." If it were not for the Master who turned me into an "upright" person, our lives and our family would probably have gone down the drain. So my husband has always been grateful to the Master. Originally a Catholic, now he is also the Master's disciple.

Later on I thought to myself, "If I could give up drinking, I would truly be making a new start." So, not long after I took refuge, I quit both drinking and smoking. My husband was very surprised and could not believe it. From that time on, I started to change. It wasn't easy to change my bad habits. But I always remembered the Master's words, "Try your best!" I never again went out singing, drinking, and dancing. Gradually, I stopped going out with those friends. I also tried to influence them by urging them to eat vegetarian food. Many of those friends we used to go out with are now Buddhists. Since they came from a variety of different backgrounds, I could only influence them to change with my own conduct.

However, I still could not switch to a completely vegetarian diet. When I went to the City of Ten Thousand Buddhas, I would sneak out for fried chicken every afternoon. How did I become a complete vegetarian? Well, at that time, the Master had just bought an old church on Sixth Street. He was about to start renovating the old building into a Way-place. That was right after the Golden Dragon Massacre of the China Youth gang. There had always been gang wars in Chinatown. Two large gangs, China Youth and Joe Boys, open fired on each other in Golden Dragon Restaurant and killed a lot of people. It made the international news. The economy of Chinatown had always depended on tourism, but with this news, the entire San Francisco Chinatown suddenly became a ghost town. No one dared to go there. People knew for sure that the China Youth gang would fight back, but they didn't know when.

The leader of the China Youth gang at that time is now the Master's disciple. One day, when they were searching for weapons, they came to the vicinity of the City of Ten Thousand Buddhas. The City was holding a Dharma assembly that day, and there were many Chinese attending. I was working as an usher by the gate. Upon spotting those young men, I warmly greeted them and led them into the City to join the Dharma assembly. The Master was holding a refuge ceremony. I didn't know who they were, but when they asked to see the Master, I was very pleased, thinking that they already wanted to learn Buddhism and take refuge with the Master at such a young age.

When the Master saw them, he asked me, "Do you know who they are?" I said, "No." When they requested to take refuge with the Master, the Master asked them very sternly, "I will grant your request, but can you stop killing, stealing, robbing, and plundering from now on?" While I was wondering why the Master was asking them so many times, they all answered, "Yes," and the Master allowed them to take refuge. After they left, the Master told me, "Those young men are members of the China Youth gang." The Master knew! But I hadn't known; and in my ignorance, I had taken them to see the Master.

Because of that event, the Master not only changed the lives of those people, he also saved the community of overseas Chinese in San Francisco. After the Golden Dragon Massacre, Chinatown had fallen into a predicament. If people continued to stay away from Chinatown, there would be no business to do.

After the members of the China Youth gang had taken refuge with the Master, they reformed, and there was no more bloodshed or gunfights. Chinatown gradually flourished again, but very few knew what had happened. The members of China Youth later helped out with many things at Gold Mountain Monastery. At that time, the City of Ten Thousand Buddhas was building its mountain gate, and they went to take charge of the work. Later, they also came to help renovate the church on Sixth Street. When Guo Gao and I brought lunch to them, I discovered that these young people of the China Youth gang were all vegetarians. I felt very ashamed and unsettled, because although I had followed the Master for many years, as their big Dharma sister, I still hadn't become completely vegetarian. One night, I was startled awake, and I seemed to hear either myself or Guan Yin Bodhisattva say, "Haven't you eaten enough?" I rushed to the Buddha hall in our home and prayed to the Bodhisattva. I rarely plead with the Bodhisattva. Even when I am seriously ill and in pain, I still feel that these are karmic obstacles which I must endure. This was the first time that I sought Guan Yin Bodhisattva's aid to help me switch to an all-vegetarian diet. The next morning, I told my husband I was going to be a vegetarian from that day on, but he didn't believe me. He said, "You must mean you will be vegetarian for today." That was when Gold Wheel Monastery was having its Opening Light Ceremony (January 2, 1983).

From that time on, I started bowing the Ten Thousand Buddhas Repentance every morning in my home, to repent of the evil karma I created in the past. The hardest thing to change has been my bad temper. When the Master used to come to Los Angeles to lecture on the Sutras every month, he would always ask me, "Do you still have a temper?" I'm still working hard on this.

The Master teaches us to change from within, not to seek outside. If we cannot even become good people, how can we become Buddhas? Therefore, we have to watch our behavior in our daily lives. We must always be alert and ask ourselves: "Is this what a Buddhist should do? Are we the Master's disciples? Have we really observed the Six Great Principles of no fighting, no greed, no seeking, no selfishness, no pursuit of personal benefit, and no lying?"

Editor's Note:

Every time there is a Sutra lecture delivered at the City of Ten Thousand Buddhas, the main gate of the City is locked. On Guanyin Bodhisattva's birthday, the nineteenth of the sixth lunar month in 1974, at approximately one o'clock in the afternoon, the Venerable Master was delivering a lecture on the "Universal Door Chapter" in the Hall of Ten Thousand Buddhas. Since there are no windows in the Hall, there is no way to see the main gate in the distance. The Venerable Master, without rising from his seat, suddenly told the Bhikshu Heng Lai to open the main gate, saying, "There are over ten people who have been waiting for a long time by the main gate. Quickly go and open the gate to let them in." Dharma Master Heng Lai did not believe what he heard at first, but when he opened the gate, indeed there were more than ten young men outside; they had been waiting for over an hour.

Upasika Helen Woo led them to offer incense in the Buddha Hall and urged them take refuge in the Triple Jewel. Although the Venerable Master had never met these people before, he knew at a glance who they were. So the Venerable Master's first words were, "If you want to take refuge, then you must not kill people, set fires, rob, engage in sexual misconduct, or take intoxicants." Everyone in the assembly was dumbstruck. They had no idea why the Venerable Master had spoken this way, and no one dared to ask those young men what they were up to. Then the Venerable Master immediately asked, "Who is the leader? Raise your hand!" The leader of the China Youth gang raised his hand.

Not long after they had taken refuge, some of the members rebelled and wished to return to their old lifestyle. That very night, however, all eight of them had the same dream—in their dream, they saw the Venerable Master appear before them and prohibit them from continuing to perpetrate evil. When they woke up the next day, they related their dreams to one another; and after that, none of them ever dared to do a bad deed again. They mended their ways, renewed themselves, and became devoted Buddhists.

It is indeed difficult to influence evil people. If it were not for the Venerable Master's personal cultivation of the Way and for his great virtue, this could hardly have happened!

HOW DOES THE MASTER CROSS OVER WESTERNERS?

ᘓ Shr Heng Liang

I was given a topic, "How is it that the Venerable Master can cross over Westerners and how is it that he can educate people?" The Master, wherever he went, any place in the world or beyond the world, whenever he encountered a living being, he could fully understand that living being. He could recognize each and every one of us. He could know our past causes and conditions and our future Buddhahood. He could know the best and the worst of each one of us. The wonderful thing about drawing near to the Master was that he helped us to recognize our worst, but at the same time he was able to bring out the very best in each of us. He did this in many ways. He did this by his adorned, pure appearance; by the words he said, which were always true; and through his deeds of virtue, which were uncountable.

He taught and transformed living beings with his every breath, with every pulse of his blood and every beat of his heart. Yet he never sought a reward of any kind—not only fame or money—he never even sought for anyone to recognize how much he was doing for living beings. He called himself an ant and a mosquito and the stupidest of people. Now, our first impression might be, "Well, an ant or a mosquito is just a very tiny, insignificant living being. That must be what the Master means." Actually, ants are very hard workers, and the Master was a very hard worker. Ants keep the earth clean of impure things; they clean away all the messes that other living beings leave. The Master cleaned up the karma of many, many living beings. An ant takes that mess on his own back and carries it away; and the Master took on the karma of many living beings. He actually took upon himself the sicknesses of many living beings. When you think of a mosquito, you think of the mosquito's never-ending sound. And that's how the Master was—he constantly spoke the Dharma; he never stopped speaking the Dharma. And he called himself the stupidest of people, because in a world where we all know how to cheat and to lie, the Master only knew how to tell the truth and how to take a loss. And just by being that way, he was able to cross over countless living beings.

People often ask how it was that the Master was able to cross over Westerners. Today I was thinking of the causes and conditions of why I left the home-life. I remember the time when I was still working in Berkeley. I had a very good job and was in a good situation. Once I went into a store to buy a pair of socks. I started writing out a check, and the salesperson told me that in order to cash my check, she needed my fingerprints. At that point I decided the world was becoming too complicated. That was around the time when I started thinking that I wanted to do something else. That was also around the time when I met the Master. The Master, compared to this modern world of asphalt and steel and computers and atomic bombs, is an oasis of compassion. He is a forest of humaneness, and he emphasizes simply being human. He emphasizes the human qualities, and he teaches us that to become a Buddha and to become fully enlightened, we need to perfect ourselves as people. Now, the Master didn't go to the United States to become famous as a Dharma Master who crosses over Americans. He simply took up his responsibility. Because the Master was a very responsible person and a very responsible cultivator, when people take refuge with the

Master, he takes complete responsibility for them and for their future as potential Buddhas. And he takes on a lot of karma. I remember, as an example of this, once in the City of Ten Thousand Buddhas, a Bhikshuni had made a mistake, and she broke the precepts. She was taught by the Master, as we all were, to confess her mistake and to repent and reform. She knelt in the Buddha hall in the midst of the great assembly and before the Master, and she repented, and then the Master, sitting on the high seat, looked down at her and said sternly, "What you have done will cause you to fall in the hells." Because this Bhikshuni truly believed in the Master, she was very afraid. She asked, "What can I do to save myself?" The Master said, with a very broad smile on his face, "I have a way to save you. I can go to the hells myself in your place and undergo the retribution for you." She couldn't accept that, of course, but the Master had already said that he would do it.

Another time, another Bhikshuni told me that one night she was very, very sick and couldn't stop vomiting. She very much believed in the Master, and so she bowed before his picture and prayed to the Master and asked him to bless her and take away her suffering. Then suddenly she felt well, and that night she had a good rest. The next morning she went to a refuge ceremony where the Master was transmitting the three refuges and the five precepts. After he had transmitted the refuges, he turned to the Bhikshuni and said, "This morning has been very difficult for me, because last night I suddenly became very ill and I vomited all night long, and so today I have no strength." That Bhikshuni knew very clearly that the Master had simply taken her suffering onto himself. Many people wonder how was it that the Master could become so ill and how could he have left us the way he did. But many of us who have been with him through the years know, and we know what a great debt of kindness we have to pay the Master. And the only way to do that is to try our very best to cultivate.

THE
BODHISATTVA'S
COMPASSION

og   Shr Heng Shou

In the early spring of 1974 I was living in Hong Kong at the Buddhist Lecture Hall when the Master returned after many years in America.

Shortly after the Master returned to Hong Kong, his disciples requested that he perform a Liberating Life Ceremony at Western Bliss Gardens, one of the temples he had founded years ago. Along with two other monks, I assisted with the chanting and playing of the Dharma instruments as the Master led the ceremony in the midst of a large crowd of lay disciples. The beings released that day were a kind of small bird whose flesh was used in Chinese cooking. A little way into the ceremony, on turning my head to pick up any ceremonial cues, I observed the Master standing next to the cages of birds. To my great surprise I noticed that he was weeping. There was no apparent statement of anguish. In fact his countenance was almost placidly and blissfully neutral. But still, there was no mistake about the fact that he really was weeping. Naturally, I was somewhat bewildered.

Since I had met the Master in the early summer of 1968, I had witnessed him displaying nearly every emotion in the course of his work as a Bodhisattva and spiritual instructor. I had seen him speaking very softly and gently to very timid disciples, at which times his voice would sound as comforting as the quiet purr of a kitten. I had seen him speak very harshly

19

and powerfully to very arrogant disciples. At those times his voice could sound as terrifying as the roar of a lion. Sometimes he would tell jokes to lighten a disciple's overly leaden mood. Sometimes he would be very stern in discouraging frivolousness where there was inattention to important details. Sometimes his presence was so beatific that everyone in his presence enjoyed a state of nearly intoxicating blissfulness even without him speaking a word. Sometimes his demeanor was so grave that anyone present spontaneously experienced a sort of glacial solemnity.

So, anyway, I had seen all of these "emotions" in the Master and in many different permutations. But I had never seen the Master weeping. I felt rather disturbed by what I had seen, but of course forged on with the rest of the ceremony, chanting and beating the wooden fish. When the ceremony came to an end, I turned and looked again at the Master who was now smiling radiantly through the traces of his recent tears. I had not been the only one who had noticed the Master weeping. In fact, I think nearly everyone was a bit confused. Then the Master offered a brief explanation (which I paraphrase here), saying, "Some of you probably noticed that I was crying as we were performing the Liberating Life Ceremony and you may have wondered why. Well, I'll tell you. The reason I wept was that I realized that one of these birds had been a monastic disciple of mine in a previous life. But this monastic strayed from the path, and eventually strayed so far that now he has taken rebirth as a bird. It was because of that that I couldn't help but weep out pity."

That ceremony at Western Bliss Gardens was an unforgettable experience for me. That he would be brought to tears over the karmic fate of one of his disciples shows the depth and genuineness of his concern for them. That he was weeping for a little bird shows me that the Master's compassion is so far-reaching that it really does extend to all living beings.

DISTANT
MEMORIES
FROM
THE BUDDHIST
LECTURE HALL

ೞ   Tim Testu (Kuo Yu)

I was intrigued by the Abbot. The ordinary things he did made such a profound impact on me that I often found myself weeping with joy. And he was very, very funny.

One afternoon a very deliberate and hard-looking woman, with a bunch of tough-looking friends in tow, came in for the Master's Sutra lecture. Their vibes were bad. These people did not appear sincere; they looked angry. One wore a leather belt with chrome spikes sticking out. The Abbot, long-since accustomed to strange-looking Westerners, spoke the Dharma in his usual manner, and when finished, asked if anyone had questions. The woman stood up.

"I have two questions," she announced. "First of all, this world has millions of people who are starving to death. Every day thousands die of hunger. What does Buddhism think about this? And what is your position in this regard?

"Secondly, the world is filled with implements of nuclear destruction. The major powers have way more weapons than they'll ever need, enough to blow up the whole world many times over, yet there never seems to be enough. What do you think should be done about all this?"

The Abbot smiled patiently and waited for the translator to repeat the question. After a short silence he calmly replied with his delightful deadpan humour, "There's really a single solution to both of these problems. Take all the extra bombs and drop them on the overpopulated areas." The women gasped in shock. Everyone else roared with laughter.

But then the Master went on to answer what was undoubtedly the real issue. He said that basically there is no problem, and that is the official Buddhist position. Unfortunately, however, people are not satisfied with this state, so they go out and create problems for themselves where originally none existed. Basically everything is okay, but we make it not okay. The point of Buddhism is for each of us to try to reach this special state of "no problem." When we are able to dwell in the midst of all problems and at the same time realize there are no problems, then we've arrived. Buddhism, for the most part, remains apolitical.

When the lecture ended, everyone seemed satisfied with the answer.

The incident reminded me of the line in the Tennessee Williams movie, "Night of the Iguana." Richard Burton asks Ava Gardner why her Chinese cook always says "*Mei you wen ti*!" every time he is asked a question or told something to do.

Ava throws back her head and laughs. "*Mei you wen ti?*" she says. "That's 10,000 years of Chinese philosophy in two words!"

"Really? Well, what exactly do those two words mean?" asks Richard.

"No problem!" smiles Ava.

On another beautiful summer afternoon, after the noisy rhythm and clatter of ceremonies, when everyone was settled in elbow-to-elbow for the lecture, I overheard the Abbot quietly turn to layman Jones and tell him to keep a particularly close eye on people. He warned him to carefully watch the door because there was someone in the building who planned on stealing.

Jones seemed to quickly forget what the Master had said, but I didn't. Maybe I felt the Abbot was also talking to me—he had a way of doing that. His mind was not singularly impeded like the rest of ours. He was aware of his connections and could read people from the inside. I was now sure of this powerful wisdom and looked for it in everything he said.

When the lecture ended, the ancient hall erupted into the usual hubbub of chitchat and socializing. Sure it was outflowing, a big release of energy, but folks just felt too darn high to contain themselves. While everyone indulged in their tête-à-tête, including Jones who'd forgotten what the Master had told him, I noticed a middle-aged Asian woman sneak into the vestibule off the main hall and try to rifle the donation box. It was like a living dream: first the prophecy, then the reality. The Master's mind flowed in and out of the future seamlessly, and he was taking us all along for the ride.

I alerted Jones, who quickly rushed in, grabbed the money from her hands, and shooed her out of the temple. The Master had already gone to his tiny room behind the altar, but his words echoed in my mind. He knew what this person was going to do before she did it! Amazing! It was as natural for the Master to read her mind, or my mind, or anyone's mind, as it was for me to speak English. How did he do it? And why was he revealing himself to me? Would I be able to do this kind of stuff if I cultivated? These incidents caused my heart of faith to grow astronomically. I really believed in Buddhism. I decided I was going to learn more about this amazing Abbot and his wondrous Buddhadharma.

One day, just to start the ball rolling, I informed the head monk that I wanted to become a disciple of the Master and that I wanted to take the five precepts. He informed the Master of my intentions. A couple of days later the Abbot approached me and said there was going to be a "Take Refuge" ceremony in a few minutes.

He asked me if I really wanted to do it. I told him I was sure. He smiled and returned to his room.

The ceremony was about to begin when one of the American monks came rushing out and informed me that if I wanted to take refuge I'd have to shave my beard.

Now, I had grown quite attached to my beard in the short time I'd had it. It made me seem tough and masculine. Dark and curly, it was part of my chosen identity. Suddenly I was forced to make a choice. What was more important: some scruffy facial hair, or taking refuge with the Everlasting Triple Jewel? I quickly ran into the bathroom and shaved off my beard—I even gave my long hair a trim. When I came out, the ceremony was up and running.

A couple of other Americans also took refuge. The Abbot, using some method known only by himself, gave us names from a choice of about 50,000 Chinese characters. I'd noticed that it was uncanny the way the names somehow applied to the people who received them. For example, one disciple was named Kuo Li. He didn't know what it meant, but after the ceremony he gave the Master a present of lapis lazuli, a precious stone he had kept in his private collection for many years. No one knew he had the stone, or that he was going to give it to the Master. Later, when he looked up his name in the Chinese dictionary, he found that it meant lapis lazuli!

I took refuge with the Buddha, the Dharma, and the Sangha, choosing the Master as my teacher, and was given the name Kuo Yü (He who goes beyond the limit). I loved my new name and was very proud of it, for I had gone beyond the limit all my life and didn't plan on stopping now. After the ceremony, a bunch of Cantonese ladies were milling around the hall. The Master came out, and they drew near him like iron filings to a magnet.

The Master looked at me and started laughing.

"Look at this stupid Westerner!" He said. "He just shaved off his nice beard so he could take refuge with me. Ha!" My face stung with embarrassment, but there was nothing I could do to bring back the beard. I sulked over to a meditation pad to hide my feelings. I'm sure I felt a chunk of my ego fall off. My identity was going south, and there was little to take its place.

Over time I found the Abbot to be very gentle with most people, but there were a few he had to lay into. That's when I heard the expression, "First comes the honeymoon, then comes the Dharma!" He taught each one of us according to our individual natures, using "no fixed Dharma," employing a radically nondogmatic approach within the framework of a highly traditional religion.

"Why is there wisdom?" He often asked. "Because the stupid make their mark!"

Using this principle, the Master challenged our ignorant actions. We created the ignorance from nothing, and the Master responded from the depths of Wisdom Store. And he certainly didn't explain all his unusual techniques. One minute he'd scold someone at the top of his voice, the next instant he'd gently inquire of someone else. Most people's emotions ran like hot and cold water from a tap.

The Master tried, it seemed, to lure us into the inconceivable ground of enlightenment beyond opposites. His occasional anger, if that's what one could call it, seemed real, yet he had no attachment to it. He could burst forth with tremendous blasts of power, shaking the windows and rattling the walls, and then relinquish it all the moment it left his lips. He went after our attachments, not our being; our self, not our Self-Esteem; our ghosts, not our Buddha-nature. We were volunteers—this was no place to take things personally. The Master performed Perfect Wisdom Mirror Service, helping us view our selves truly for the first time. He once conceded that his job was to get us oscillating between opposites: between good and bad, fear and love, happy and sad, inside and out, so on and so forth, until we got to where we no longer lurked in the illusions of opposites, the world of dualities, the idea of a separate self in an "outside world." We had to find the middle ground that was no ground in our true self-nature that was no self-nature.

The Master made free use of what he called his "radar" to teach from "the inside out." This put him universes beyond other so-called "masters" who tried to teach from the outside in. How could they possibly teach when they didn't have the ability to see what their disciples were doing behind their backs?

"Don't get the wrong impression," the Master said. "I'm really a nobody, a big nothing, a living dead man. You all want to be first, number one. I want to be last. You all are so smart, while I am cultivating my way to stupidity.

Just remember, you can cheat your teacher, you can cheat yourself, but you can't cheat the Buddhas and Bodhisattvas. If you want to try, however, go ahead and check it out."

He gave the Buddhas and Bodhisattvas credit for everything.

Small Novice was an American disciple who received a lot of verbal "beatings." This poor fellow had particular difficulty following the rules and stopping his outflows. One night, as the story goes, Small Novice became filled with the desire to go "outside" and do something. Now, many of us had wrestled with that one, but he actually decided to act upon it. Donning civilian clothes, including a wool cap to cover his bald head, Small Novice slid down a drain pipe from the fourth floor balcony, landed on a third floor balustrade, and fled down the fire escape into the night. He was gone several hours doing God knows what. Just before morning services he snuck back into the building the same way he went out.

No one saw him leave, no one saw him return, and he told no one about his big adventure.

The next day, however, the Master approached him and asked, "Where did you go last night?"

"Nowhere, Shrfu," replied the trembling monk.

"Then what were you doing on the bus?" inquired the Abbot. As always, whenever the Abbot spoke, everyone in the little room listened intently. This was definitely going to be another teaching experience.

"I, I, I, don't know," cried the Novice.

"Just who is it that doesn't know?" yelled the Abbot.

"I, I, I don't know."

"Who gave you the cigarette?"

"I, I can't remember," wailed the monk.

"Why were you talking to that girl on the bus?"

Small Novice's face turned deep purple. "How did you know?" he cried in astonishment.

"How do I know?" yelled the Abbot. "I'll tell you how I know…. Did you know?"

The young monk looked flabbergasted.

"Well, did you know?" the Abbot yelled again.

"Yes."

"Then that's how I know!" There was a prolonged silence.

"Just remember!" counselled the Abbot, "You may be able to cheat yourself, but you can't cheat the Great Assembly!"

The Master explained to us that in the golden age of Buddhism, during the T'ang dynasty, teachers had to beat their disciples into enlightenment. He said, however, that in America we were too soft, and Buddhism was too new. There was no way he could physically beat us, even though he was sure we needed it, and that undoubtedly it would do us some good. If he did, we'd all just run away, so his "beatings" would have to be mental, mind to mind. Just like the Patriarchs, but without the stick. If we wanted to get enlightened and obtain Samadhi, we'd have to toughen up and learn to take it. Most of us really wanted these "beatings." The Master's verse addressed this principle, and he repeated it to us over and over again.

> *Everything is a test*
> *To see what you will do;*
> *If you don't recognize what's before your face*
> *Then you must start anew.*

The Master informed us that in the future he might test us. We wouldn't know if it was real or a test, however, because he wasn't going to explain everything—we'd have to do our own figuring out. Some of these tests would be very hard to take, he warned, but we shouldn't fear a little suffering. Most of us would run away, he predicted, but that was no problem. We could run all we wanted—there was no way out of the universe. When we got tired, he'd be waiting for us; his door was open. He would neither beg us to come in, nor ask us to leave.

Some of the elder disciples asked if they could test the newer people to "help" them along the road to enlightenment. The Master blasted that false thinking, saying that he would be the only one making up the tests. Besides, most tests would arise of themselves, from within and without. If we didn't pass them, we'd get to start anew.

Furthermore, our enlightenment, should we ever experience it in this lifetime, wouldn't be considered genuine unless certified by a true Master, a Master certified by the lineage of sages reaching back to the original teacher, Shakyamuni Buddha.

Thus, if we wanted it, we were going to get it. Those who stayed could count on being "beaten," cajoled, pushed, pulled, inspired, and empowered into enlightenment. No need for fear. Most of us recognized the beatings as manifestations of the highest form of compassion.

Those who kept an open mind, who patiently practised, and who acted sincerely would get a response—a response exactly commensurate with the practice. Those who stuck around would experience incredible states, see things never before seen, and have some awfully rocky territory to navigate on the road to enlightenment. Like many others who arrived at the Buddhist Lecture Hall in the late sixties and early seventies, I carried with me a lot of bad habit energy. Actually, I had them all beat in that department. But thanks to the Master, most of us were able to give up drinking, smoking, drugs, meat-eating and many other dark attachments. To help displace this ugly *Ch'i*, the Master filled our minds with ancient words of wisdom: the teachings of the Patriarchs, Ch'an talks, words of Dharma.

The meditation periods worked hand in hand with the talks to bring about a centering effect, a vacuum of emptiness into which the teachings could flow. Just by sitting still, the six senses—the abilities to see, hear, smell, taste, touch, and think—became pure and enhanced. Perhaps we'd develop psychic powers, attain the ability to see into the past and future, or be able to read people's minds. Most of all, we had the opportunity to enter Samadhi, experience Satori, an apercu—to become Buddhas.

To get there, however, we'd have to go far beyond the nonchalant, McDonald's-type meditations so popular in America, the kind where people dozed off in chairs with their legs dangling down. Sure, these methods could make a person feel better.

They provided a nice little battery charge. But how could anyone have the gall to market short naps? Our Abbot was teaching the incredible process leading to the ending of the cycle of birth and death.

After innumerable hours of sitting, the muscles and tendons in my legs gradually rearranged themselves. On occasion, I could sit for the full hour in half lotus, even though it was painful, and every once in a while I could twist into full lotus for a few minutes. Still, the waves of false thought arose from nowhere, and I continued to be lost in them.

Helpless to stop this spurious flow, I indulged in trying to sort things out. I spent countless hours trying to make sense of my life, but the thoughts continued to flow like smoke from a fire. I'd follow one particle up until it disappeared, and then immediately grasp onto the next ash that came floating by.

I tried regulating my breath, counting my breath, reciting special mantras, staring at the floor, rolling my eyeballs, and everything else I could think of, but my brains just kept smoking away.

Eventually, however, I discovered some techniques for clearing the mind. Shrfu taught us the sweeping dharma. When thoughts popped up, rather than get lost in them, we could brush them away. This was very subtle and difficult work. Sometimes the thoughts seemed quite profound, and indeed they were, but as far as meditation goes, they were just more dust, so we swept them away and they lost their power over us.

All these changes, of course, were happening in a very short period of time. I wasn't really aware of how these processes were working.

We weren't just "studying" Buddhism, we were living it, and even though just beginners, were already reaping some of the rewards of practice.

The Abbot devoted his primary energy to the left-home people. We laypersons were free to learn from them and to benefit from their mistakes; they made plenty. The Abbot alternated between building them up, nourishing their egos and attachments, and then letting them fall back down, leaving only, one hoped, a shiny Buddha-nature. It was certainly fun to watch. Sometimes he'd pick a tiny little thing they'd done, and then seem to blow it all out of proportion. No one, for example, could ever forget the famous cottage cheese incident, when a tall, silver-tongued American monk manipulated a laywoman into offering some cottage cheese. For the next few weeks the Master would resurrect the incident again and again to drive his point home, showing us how the monk was acting like a "*P'an Yuan* (Climbing on Conditions) Ghost," and how we were all caught up in the three evils of greed, hatred, and stupidity. The way to get rid of those evils was by practicing morality, concentration, and wisdom. In the midst of all this serious teaching we'd often be laughing through rivers of joyous tears.

The monks and nuns had put themselves in a position to be taught. They had no beards, no hair, no clothes, no money, no anything. They'd taken a giant leap of faith, leaving the world and its dust behind. I was a little jealous. I wanted special attention from the Master; I ached for it. For the time being, however, I contented myself with just sitting back and watching the show. My brief moment in the spotlight would come.

The Abbot especially encouraged his monks and nuns to cultivate the "Awesome Manner." "Don't walk around with your heads lowered, going 'Mee-mee, moo-moo'!" Don't act like a bunch of frogs!" he said. "Walk tall and proud, be fierce and fearless, and emit blazing light. Walk like the wind! Sit like a bell! Stand like a pine!" The Abbot certainly demonstrated The Awesome Manner himself. Though his mind was still, many people trembled when in his presence. This was because of their demons within.

Those with a pure mind, with nothing to hide or be ashamed of, had no trouble being around the Master.

The American monks and nuns could sit in full lotus without moving for the full hour meditations. I was still scared of the sitting meditation pain. I didn't feel I'd ever make a breakthrough. When it was 10:00 PM and lights out, I was ready to lie down and stretch those legs; I had my limits. These other people seemed to never stop cultivating. Even at night, when they were allowed to sleep, they'd stay up into the wee hours working on translations. And all this on only one meal a day!

Although Buddhism was now my religion of choice, it occurred to me that I didn't have to turn my back on Christianity. On the contrary, by following the precepts of Buddhism, I had become a better Christian than ever. For one thing, I was not "living in sin," but learning to "know, love, and serve God." My whole idea of God changed, however. I no longer thought of "Him" as some eighty-foot tall, long-haired guy in the sky, but as a cosmic force pervading me and the universe, a force beyond all opposites, including birth and death, with which I would have a chance to reunite if I practiced the principles of Buddhism. Why wait to go to heaven; I could experience God and "heaven" right in this life. We didn't have to be lambs any longer; in Buddhism we could be lions. I liked the idea of faith, practice, and results in this life. But Christianity had its wonderful purpose in the world, and most religions had the power to help people grow spiritually. Even groups as radical as the Hare Krishna were taking druggies off the streets and making them clean up their act, eat vegetables, and start thinking of someone else besides themselves. Shrfu taught us that all these religions were lights taking away the darkness of the world. So I gratefully took the love, compassion, knowledge and wisdom bestowed on me from all the virtuous nuns, brothers, priests, and my good Catholic family, and used it as a foundation for Buddhist studies.

At the Buddhist Lecture Hall we were free to create our own spiritual program from 84,000 mysterious Dharma Doors. The Master encouraged us to see through everything as false, illusory, and empty, and asked that we let go of it all, even to the point of letting go of Buddhism. "There are no fixed Dharmas!" he often said. "Your mind should be like empty space." So, with my heart resolved on Bodhi, I let go of my past and moved forward into territory unknown. Together, with brothers and sisters of like mind, I was on an extraordinary journey to the roots of consciousness. Each of us alone, yet together, shared a common bond of faith. It was, as the Abbot taught, our good roots and our vows from past lives bringing us back together. We were extremely fortunate to meet with this opportunity. We were all on a spiritual roll and the Abbot was blowing people's minds, tirelessly turning the awesome Dharma Wheel, sharing this magnificent treasure with everyone.

I DON'T HAVE
THE SLIGHTEST
SPECK
OF DESIRE

ଓ Shr Heng Shun

The Venerable Master's state is something that cannot be fathomed by even Arhats of the fourth stage of Enlightenment who have already transcended the cycle of birth and death. So how can we common people understand him? (The Master said this on August 6, 1974 during a Chan session a few days after I had started to live at Gold Mountain Monastery.)

In 1986 when the Master made what I believe was his first visit to Indonesia—one morning the Master came out of his room and looked at a Dharma brother and myself and said, "You don't have the slightest idea about what I am about." I'm afraid that the situation today, as I write these words, is still quite the same.

In late 1976 or early 1977, after I had first become a Bhikshu, the Master once told me as I knelt before him in his guest room, "I don't have the slightest speck of desire." The Master said this in his very calm ocean-like voice as he held his thumb and forefinger together signalling a speck. I know that the Master was speaking about a reality that was his normal experience.

The Master influences people more than anything else with his everyday behavior. For approximately fifteen years I was in constant close contact with the Master. Whenever I had a problem, there is always a memory of the Master doing or saying something which resolved the problem.

During that time one thing which stood out for me about the Master was his vigor. No matter what we were doing or where we were going, the Master was always reciting. Whether he was reciting mantras or Sutras or both doesn't matter. The Master always cultivated with incredible vigor. He said never neglect your "homework," meaning cultivation, no matter what you are doing.

When he was lecturing the *Flower Adornment Sutra* he said that even in his sleep he would be reciting that Sutra.

The Master's teaching is so difficult to fathom. Once he continuously reprimanded a young American resident at the old Gold Mountain Monastery to stop looking around at this and that all the time. He reprimanded the thirteen or fourteen year old like this for a year or two. Then one day the Master told the boy, who by then was a little novice, that from then on it was his job to look at everyone who came through the door for the evening lecture on the *Flower Adornment Sutra*. As soon as he obeyed the Master's instructions, his spiritual eye opened and the Master would often have him describe what he saw during the lectures to the assembly.

Now would it work that way with us? Of course not. This just shows how dynamic and alive the Master's lectures were. The interaction of the Enlightened Master's mind with that of his faithful students is not something one can read in a book.

The only text I can think of which aptly describes this state is in the "Dharma Realm Chapter" in the twenty-first roll of the *Flower Adornment Sutra*. It relates the pilgrimage of the pure youth Good Wealth and his visits to fifty-three Good Spiritual Counselors. The visits represent the inconceivable interaction of Enlightened Bodhisattvas with great vows and accumulated good karma with the affinities and karma of the youth.

Each taught him differently and represented a certain level on the path to Enlightenment. Yet these levels were not levels that they were limited to, rather it was merely the way their karmic affinities played out with those of Good Wealth's. So it is with the Master's interaction with the literally measureless people and other beings who had the good fortune/ karma to meet or be taught by him.

Simply one teaching, like the Master's "Return the Light" verse, can take a person all the way. It can enable one to transcend the cycle of birth and death, and then be able to turn the wheel of wondrous Dharma for others by one's very existence. That is, one's every move and thought will then embody the Buddhadharma so that one naturally influences others. What is true is not thought about or planned. The way to truly change the world outside is only by changing one's own mind!

COMMEMORATIVE
ESSAY

୪ Martin Verhoeven
(Kuo Ting)

Like the China of Great Master Hsuan-tsang's time, America in the late 20th century is awash with a staggering variety of Buddhisms. Just as wave after wave of divergent Indian Buddhist schools and sects inundated China from the end of the Han up through the Tang, so have we witnessed in the West an equally rich and perplexing infusion of schools and teachings—all purporting to be genuine, orthodox, the "real teaching." Great Master Hsuan-tsang (c.586-664) sought to resolve the confusion of so many conflicting opinions by pilgrimaging to India to seek out the genuine Dharma for himself at its source, and to bring back the sacred scriptures to his homeland.

A great scholar and translator and one of the few Chinese to have mastered Sanskrit, Great Master Hsuan-tsang's stupendous journey marked a high point in the transmission of Buddhism from one culture to another. Americans now, like the Chinese of the Sui and Tang, long for the same clarity and voice of authority. Ironically, the venerable Hsuan-tsang may have had an easier time in his quest than contemporary seekers.

For even when the texts became readily available to Americans (available in a quantity and quality perhaps unequaled in history), the "reading" of those texts proved far more difficult and daunting than we imagined. As the Great Master Hsuan-tsang discovered, and as we Americans are belatedly discovering, Buddhism—the real and vital Buddhism—is penetrated not simply through reading texts (however carefully) and learned exegeses, but through a far more subtle and interior process called "self-cultivation." Great Master Hsuan-tsang's insight and understanding of the written discourses derived from two complementary sources: his own virtuous life of spiritual practice, and his intimate contact with genuine "good knowing advisors" (*kalamitryana*) he encountered throughout his incredible journey.

As it is said, "The Way and the response inconceivably intertwine; practice and understanding mutually respond." Reading Great Master Hsuan-tsang's journal, one cannot avoid the impression that "good knowing advisors," true personifications of the Buddha-Way, were more numerous and accessible then than now. Moreover, in perhaps that less materialistic and "primitive" time, love of one's spiritual nature seemed more cherished; self-cultivation more refined. Thus, although our libraries and bookstores abound with Buddhist texts and works on Buddhism, our knowledge of, and more significantly our cultivation of, that sacred teaching does not for all of that seem proportionately advanced. Nor does our desire for the "unsurpassed, wonderful Dharma" seem as hungry as that of the men and women who lived centuries before ours.

Another irony: Where Great Master Hsuan-tsang had to risk life and limb traversing god-forsaken deserts and freezing mountains to find the teachings of enlightenment and wise mentors, we in America find both teachings and teachers arriving practically on our doorsteps. Since the 1890s and especially since World War II, Buddhism and Buddhist masters have clearly set the Dharma on a new course: from East to West, from Asia to America. This fragile transfer of ancient wisdom to the New World, as with all previous migrations of the Dharma to new lands, however, depends for its success on transplanting not simply the scriptures, but transmitting the "living tradition." Only on the strength and inspiration of living examples of Buddhism does the Dharma take root in fresh soil and grow in new hearts. Such an exemplar was Venerable Master Hsuan Hua. And such was the scope of his vow: to bring the Dharma to America.

My first meeting with the Master in 1976 underscored the importance of the direct and personal encounter. (Interestingly, I "met" the Master in a dream months before I actually met him in San Francisco at the Gold Mountain Monastery.) As was customary and proper, nearly everyone present at the monastery that afternoon to hear him lecture, bowed to the Master, showing their respect for the Dharma he inherited and passed along. I chafed at the thought of bowing to another. "How unbecoming and demeaning," I thought as I watched others bow. "That's so self-abasing and superstitious; I would never kowtow like that to a person!" I suppose in the back of my mind stood the Christian admonition of my childhood catechism lessons not to "worship false gods."

Then during the sutra lecture, the Master, as if out of the blue, digressed in his commentary (or so it seemed) to observe that, "Some people come to the temple seeking the Way, but are so full of self and their own self-importance that they cannot receive the Way. Like a tea cup already full to the brim in which the water of Dharma only spills over the side, they only wish to be noticed, to be praised and given a 'high hat' to wear. They are arrogant and proud and so, 'having eyes they cannot see; having ears they cannot hear.'"

These words struck to my heart. I felt they were surgically directed right at me. I didn't enjoy hearing this criticism, yet strangely I didn't really mind either. Somehow hearing such an honest and direct truth about myself made me forget for the moment the sting of their bitterness to my ego.

Good medicine is bitter to the taste;
Honest words grate on the ears.

I had never before thought of myself as arrogant, but I recognized immediately the Master's skillful perception of my state of mind. After the lecture I went up to the Master and bowed. I thought to myself, "Anyone who knows me better than I know myself, deserves my respect. Truly I received an invaluable gift today from this curious monk." The Master just smiled.

I continued to come to the Master's lectures and discovered a teaching that surpassed my expectations. For the first time in my life I felt totally intellectually free to inquire and explore—without dogma, without doctrine, without creed or the abandonment of reason. The Master was then explaining the *Avatamsaka Sutra,* and I felt myself inexorably drawn into its "understanding and expanding of the mind and all its states...the unattached, unbound, liberated mind." The Master was my introduction to Buddhism; his profound and expansive teaching my understanding of what Buddhism was. That impression was shattered when I traveled to Asia the following year.

In 1977 I was part of a delegation that accompanied the Master on a lecture tour of Malaysia, Singapore, Hong Kong, Indonesia, and Thailand. I wasn't prepared for the acculturated forms of Buddhism that have come to dominate the Asian Buddhist world. Centuries of accretion, absorption, and cross-fertilization with indigenous customs and beliefs, local cults, and downright superstition has resulted in "Buddhisms" one would never find in any sutra.

In one particular temple the gaudy display and wai-tao (lit. 'outside the Way') hoopla was especially disturbing and out-of-hand. Dead ducks and bottles of wine covered the altars as offerings to the Buddha (whose precepts enjoin against intoxicants and the taking of life), choking clouds of incense smoke filled the air, making it painful to breathe and sooting the gilded images so heavily that they no longer appeared golden radiant but sticky, ocher brown. Messy oil lamps spilled all over the altars and floors as each devotee struggled to empty his or her gallon bottle into the tiny lanterns. In the corners of the temple people huddled, shaking "fortune sticks" out of cups onto the floor to divine their fate and future. Bereaved relatives burned wads of paper money to "buy off" the angry and vengeful ghosts of the underworld who they believed obstructed their departed ones from rebirth in the heavens. Outside, huge papier-mache boats, cars, houses, planes, and palaces were set to torch and "sent" to the dead to appease them and confer on them riches and wealth. The whole temple-scene resembled a circus or carnival atmosphere. There was even a Gwan-yin Bodhisattva pinball machine where for a coin one could mechanically manipulate a plastic goddess along a track to shovel out a toy ball containing a blessing or prediction of blessings and eternal reward. This was the nadir of my disillusionment with "Buddhism."

When the Master addressed the audience, however, his tone resembled the "lion's roar." With humor softening a patriarch's righteous duty to protect the Proper Dharma, he took issue with nearly everything we were witnessing in the name of Buddhism.

"If you offer a stick of incense," he began "it is symbolic—symbolic of your desire to become pure of mind and body, pure in the precepts, so as to be a worthy vessel of the Buddha-Way. Incense-lighting signifies your sincere wish to cleanse your own mind and thoughts and to evoke thereby a response from the Buddhas and Bodhisattvas. It's symbolic, a gesture. The smoke doesn't by itself 'purify' nor does it please the Buddha in the way that we people are pleased by perfume and fragrant food. To think that is to be totally confused about true principle. That actually slanders the Buddha. Think about it. How could the Buddha be the Buddha if he was still

41

'flowing in sights and smells,' still turning in the dust of the senses? Even an *arhat* has gone beyond enslavement to the senses! Do you think that if one incense stick smells good and pleases the Buddha, then a hundred will please him even more—like bribing an official with a present or enticing a child with candy? The Buddha isn't greedy for good things the way ordinary people are. To think and act that way really looks down on the Buddha." Some people began to shift nervously in their seats; others, began to sit up and take notice.

The Master continued, "Look at the Buddha statues! They're all black and tarnished from all the incense smoke! They're choking on it. Instead of a Pure Land we are creating a polluted land—all due to greed and ignorance." At this point you could hear a pin drop.

Some people, obviously offended and upset over what they were hearing, actually got up and walked out. Others, however, especially the younger and better-educated in the audience, applauded enthusiastically and beamed.

The Master went on, "Even though I do not like to speak this way, I cannot not say this. I have made a vow that as long as I have breath and can speak, the proper Dharma will not vanish from this world."

The Venerable Master continued, "As for burning paper money for ghosts, ask yourself: Is that reasonable? Does it make sense? Aren't ghosts immaterial? So what use would they have for things material, especially fake money? Even children can't be taken in by phony money; so how would ghosts who have ghostly psychic powers be fooled?! What use have the dead, whose bodies have returned to the elements, for paper houses, cars, boats, and airplanes? This is truly silly and superstitious!"

Then in a calm and compassionate voice the Master closed: "What is Buddhism? It's just the teaching of wisdom. Shakyamuni Buddha said upon his enlightenment, 'All living beings have the Buddha-nature; all can become Buddhas. It's only because of confused thinking and attachments that they don't realize the Tathagata's state.' Buddha just means 'awakened one'; so don't confuse the branches for the root; don't forsake the near-at-hand and seek far and distant. Return the light to illumine within; seek the Buddha of your mind. That's all I wish to say for now."

Next morning as I washed my face at the water sink I met the Master. He smiled and asked me, "Well, what did you think of my talk last night?"

"Well, Shifu," I replied, "it upset a lot of people, but it also made many people happy."

The Master said, "I don't speak to upset nor to please; I only speak what is true, what accords with true principle. That's all I know how to do; I have always been that way."

I then confessed my disillusionment with the Buddhism I was seeing on the tour in Asia. I told him that I expected to find the pure and lofty teaching here in the East, in the 'holy land,' so to speak, of Buddhism. But instead I encountered many of the same superstitions and strange beliefs I met in other religions. He said softy and very deliberately, "Everything is made from the mind alone. Buddhism is just the teaching of wisdom, the teaching of the mind. Buddhism is meant to liberate the mind, to activate one's inherent wisdom. I want my students to have wisdom, to discover their inner wisdom, not to become superstitious or attached. Don't follow me, don't follow him. Listen to yourself—your True Self, your Buddha-nature—learn to follow true principle and to use your own wisdom. If it's the Tao, advance; if it's not the Tao, turn back. Remember what it says in the *Vajra Sutra*: 'Those seeking me in sights or seeking me in sounds, walk a deviant path and will never find the Thus Come One.' Do you understand?" he asked with a gentle smile.

A few weeks later on the same tour I was riding with the Master in a car en route to a lecture in the countryside. The driver, a local devout layman, asked the Master, "Master, the Theravada school says there is only one Buddha, the historical Buddha. The Mahayana school says there are many Buddhas. Which is correct? Is there one Buddha or are there lots of Buddhas?" He was, it seemed, slightly baiting the Master, yet also sincere in his query.

The Master replied, "There are no Buddhas." The layman was stunned; the car jerked.

"Huh!? How can you say there are no Buddhas?!" he asked incredulously.

The Master smiled and said, "'Basically there's not one thing, so where can dust alight?' Originally there is just great wisdom. Whoever has great wisdom, whoever can find and use their innate wisdom is a Buddha. Whoever remains confused is just a living being. Potentially every living being is a Buddha. Whoever remains confused is just a living being. Potentially every living being is a Buddha, so I say there are limitless Buddhas. But Buddha just means 'awakened one.' Awakened to what? Awakened to the truth of no-self. So fundamentally you could say there are no Buddhas; all Buddhas are not." The Master paused to see if the layman understood. Then he continued, "You eat to satisfy your own hunger; you wear clothes to keep yourself warm, and you cultivate to save yourself. So whether there is one Buddha or a thousand, unless you cultivate there are still Buddhas and you are still a living being—the two are unrelated and the question of one or many is irrelevant. What do you think of my answer?"

The layman thought quietly for a long time, and then shaking his head said, "Hmm. That's really good; really good." I to myself said the same.

Finally, I remember observing the Master sitting in at a conference on children and education. Upon hearing the statistics and reports on the deteriorating condition of children throughout the world—children suffering from hunger, poverty, abuse, parental neglect, exposed to increasing levels of violence and depravity—the Master quietly bowed his head and began to softly weep. As the tears came streaming down his face, I was reminded of that other aspect of Buddhism the Master so often taught and embodied: great compassion. His deep sense of "being one with everyone" led me to imagine that his tears were no doubt for the children, and for those who hurt them, and for the children of those children yet to come. But he cried (incredibly) out of shame for his own "lack of virtue," as he would say, for not having done a good enough job in his own cultivation or by the example and output of his own life, to have prevented such a tragedy.

It was this living example of a great soul "manifesting a body to speak the Dharma," that made Buddhism come alive for me and I am sure for many others who met the Master. And it is in those meetings, those person-to-person encounters, that the Master's spirit continues to live. What he instilled by his example and tireless giving to each individual he met, insures in some ineffable way that the Dharma will continue to live—to live not just in translations, but in the boundless living beings who had the privilege and opportunity to be kindled and transformed by his light.

REMEMBRANCE
AND
GRATITUDE

og   Ron Epstein (Guo Rong)

After having been invited to the United States by some disciples from
Hong Kong, the Master established a Buddhist Lecture Hall in San
Francisco's Chinatown in 1962. In 1963, because some of the disciples
there were not respectful of the Dharma, he left Chinatown and moved the
Buddhist Lecture Hall to a first-floor flat in a rundown Victorian building
on the edge of San Francisco's Fillmore District and Japantown. The other
floors of the building contained individual rooms for rent with communal
kitchens. Those rooms were occupied by poor, elderly black people and a
bunch of young Americans who were, in various ways, eagerly searching for
meaning in their lives.

I first met the Master in January, 1966. I was a poor student in need of
a place to stay and rented a room on the second floor of the building. The
young people in the building all consciously or unconsciously knew that
the Master was a very special person, but because we knew next to nothing
about Buddhism, we had no categories to use to express our understanding
or lack of it. We knew that the Master was a Chinese Buddhist monk, but
didn't really know what that meant. One young man had actually taken
refuge with the Master, but we didn't know what that meant either, or even
whether it was different than leaving home. Basic Buddhist courtesy and

the notions of making offerings and moral precepts were totally alien to us. The Master never mentioned that he was a Patriarch and had thousands of disciples in China and Hong Kong. Many local Chinese Buddhists were angry at him for leaving Chinatown. Only a handful of the most loyal disciples would regularly come to see him and make offerings, nonetheless, the Master would share what he had with the people in the building. He would put bags of rice in the communal kitchens, so that no one would have to go hungry. Sometimes, on Buddhist holidays or when he had extra food, he would invite several of us to lunch and often prepare the food himself. We all thought the food was delicious. In those days when sometimes only one or two people who didn't even understand Chinese came to hear the Dharma, the Master lectured the same way that he did in later years when there were hundreds or even thousands. I remember going to listen to him lecture on the *Lotus Sutra*. With the same awesome demeanor that we have all come to know, he would sit at the head of two fold-out picnic tables with an ancient blackboard behind him. Often there was no one to translate, and when there was, it was usually two young high school students who could not translate very well. I didn't understand the Sutra at all, but when I went, it was to be in the Master's presence and to listen to the sound of his voice.

More popular with some of the young Americans was the Master's open meditation hour from seven to eight every evening. There were usually a few people there, and I sat with him more and more the longer I lived in the building. Although the popular San Francisco Zen Center was just a couple of blocks away, I began to be sensitive to a special quality of my meditation when in the Master's presence.

It took me about six months to have a clear realization about the Master. When it finally came, I was amazed. I still knew practically nothing about Buddhism, but I understood that the Master was like no one else I had ever met in my entire life. I saw that he was truly without any vestige of selfish individuality, and thus I could never feel any real conflict of interest with him. He knew me more deeply than I knew myself, accepted me in a way that no one else did, and was compassionately concerned about my welfare, so that there was nothing to fear from him. I sensed that he had great wisdom and special psychic power, and yet there he was every day, always appearing ordinary and entirely inconspicuous.

I suspect that the insights I had about him at that time were in no way special to me, but that something similar or even more profound was deeply felt by all those, Buddhist or not, whatever their ethnic background or education, who opened their awareness to him. A few months later, with great excitement I travelled to Asia to meet the Buddhadharma in its homeland. How strange it was for me to naively encounter for the first time the 2500-year-old shell of Buddhist institutional tradition. With precious few exceptions, I found it to be devoid of any living spirit. Shortly after my return to the United States, I entered the university world of academic Buddhist scholarship and became a graduate student first at the University of Washington and then at Berkeley. I marvelled at the extensive and keen intellectual knowledge of the Buddha's teachings possessed by some of my mentors.

Yet at the same time I wondered why almost all of them vigorously resisted allowing the living spirit of the Buddhadharma to enter their personal lives. The twofold disillusionment I experienced during those years was painful to bear. Yet perhaps for me, those difficult lessons were necessary to help me learn to cherish the rarity and the preciousness of a genuine Master. It would have been enough for me just to have had the opportunity to be in the presence of such a genuinely selfless person. Yet the Master was so much more for me and my family. We, like so many others, literally owe our physical lives to him. And he never failed to be there for us, to counsel us in times of personal crisis, and to advise us and our children. It goes without saying that we are grateful beyond words for what we received.

Equally or even more valuable to me is that he gave ultimate meaning to my life. He showed me every day in his every single action that the wonderful world of the Buddha-dharma portrayed in the Sutras is not fantasy, fairy tale or intellectual abstraction. He showed me that it is real and alive, and even more importantly, a possibility and practical ideal for our own lives. I remember him saying that we should explain the Sutras as if we ourselves had spoken them, to make them our own and not distance ourselves from them. Clearly that is the example that he expressed through his own life. The time of receiving is now over. It is time to grow up and become an adult in the Dharma. That is not easy for me, even after so many years. It is important not to be overwhelmed by the enormity of the debt owed, and the fact that, within the scope of my limited understanding, it can never be repaid. The Master always told us, "Do your best." Now more than ever before, it is time for me to do what I can, in my limited way with my limited vision, to continue his work both within myself and in this difficult world of impermanence and suffering. Although he has left his physical body, I know that the Master is still here, deep down in my heart, in the true pure land which has no inside and outside.

THE VENERABLE MASTER AS I KNEW HIM

Terri Nicholson
(Kuo Ts'an)

It is difficult to write about someone as special as the Master. The boundaries that limit most of us did not exist for him. His heart reached out and gathered in everyone—the wealthy, the poor, leaders of nations, common citizens, children, the elderly, Buddhists, Christians, Moslems, Jews, Asians, Americans, Europeans. He saw through all of the differences that come between us, deeply understood us all, and used every ounce of his energy to bring the Buddha's teachings into our hearts and expand the capacity of our minds.

Yet, to me, the most miraculous quality of the Master was his simplicity and ordinariness. All that he accomplished was done without any pretense on his part. He was always one of us. He conducted himself as an ordinary human being; never drawing attention to himself as being special or better that others. He never asked anyone to believe in him, but he did encourage us to believe in ourselves. Isn't that the most amazing thing of all, that ordinary living beings can become Buddhas?

In the over twenty years that I have been lucky enough to be his disciple, I have watched the Master forget himself completely for the sake of the Dharma and give of himself endlessly to help others. He never neglected even the tiniest thing he could do to help others, and always refused to take even a moment for himself. Yet, he was the happiest person I have ever known. It is his joy in the Dharma and his unfailing sense of humor that I treasure most in difficult times. I only pray that we can see through the illusory differences we put between ourselves and others, and repay the Master's kindness by working together and delighting in the joy of the Dharma.

I heard him speak of pulling weeds in the street,
Of cleaning toilets with his bare hands,
Of doing what others could not do.
Not just once—many times.

I saw him get out of the car after traveling for hours,
And not stop to rest even for a moment,
Before coming to speak the Dharma.
Not just once—many times.

I watched him give away whatever he could to others—
Food, clothing, happiness,
Even the City of Ten Thousand Buddhas
    he gave to all living beings.
He gave whatever made others happy,
Not just once—many times.

I got to be there when he made big problems seem small,
And little problems disappear,
Sometimes only with a smile or a few words,
Not just once—many times.

I watched him bring people together that others
    swore could not get along,
East and West, North and South,
And they worked together,
Not just once—many times.

A CAMPHOR
TREE WAITS
1989 YEARS
TO TAKE
REFUGE

Plants want to take refuge too?

In the countyard of Universal Salvation Monastery on Potola Mountain of Zhejiang Province in China, a 1989 - year old camphor tree, through a person with spiritual power, requested to take refuge with the Venerable Master.

Long Beach Monastery, facing the Pacific Ocean, is the second Buddhist Way-place that the Master established in southern California, after Gold Wheel Monastery in Los Angeles. On October 23, 1994, the weather was ideal. At 8:00 am twenty-one Buddhist disciples who were preparing to shave their heads, along with 300 other Buddhists, participated in a bowing ceremony, which preceded the ceremony for entering monastic life.

Among the twenty-one people who resolved to leave the home life, four were male and seventeen, female. They came from Finland, Canada, the United States, China, Taiwan, Hong Kong, Singapore, Malaysia, and Vietnam. Their ages ranged from six to seventy-two.

Following the ceremony for entering monastic life, the transmission of the three refuges, five precepts, and ten novice precepts were held in the afternoon. During these ceremonies a special overseas call came from China to the Master. The Master's disciple, Upasaka Yang, related the following true account:

When my father and I were visiting Potola Mountain, at Universal Salvation Monastery, we saw a camphor tree that was so huge it would have taken ten people hand-in-hand to encircle it. That tree spoke to me, saying it wanted to take refuge with the Venerable Master Hsuan Hua. I found this quite odd and asked the tree, "You've been in this monastery for so many years. Haven't you met a true cultivator and taken refuge? Why do you want to take refuge with the Master?" The tree said that he had never met a real cultivator with whom he could take refuge, that the conditions had not ripened before, and that now he hoped to take refuge with the Master. I said, "Fine! Wait until I ask the Master. I'll let you know."

Later, I went back to my room and fell asleep, exhausted. When I woke up, I had forgotten all about this matter. I had neither told my father nor asked the Master about it. We were going to visit other monasteries in the afternoon. When we got downstairs, I turned around to talk to my father. All of a sudden, I sprained my neck. Fortunately, it did not break. I was immediately alert, "What did I do wrong?" Just as I was pondering, I turned around and saw the big camphor tree and instantly realized that I had forgotten to do what he had asked me to do. Just then, the tree said to me, "How could you be so careless and forget what I asked you to do?"

"I'm so sorry! My memory is very poor. Please don't be upset. I will ask the Master now." So I asked the Master for instruction.

The Master said, "Whether or no he becomes my disciple is not important, but he should diligently cultivate precepts, samadhi, and wisdom and put to rest greed, hatred, and delusion."

I relayed the message to the camphor tree and added, "As long as you can observe the Six Principles of the City of Ten Thousand Buddhas: no fighting, no greed, no seeking, no selfishness, no pursuit of self-benefit, and no lying, then even if you don't have the affinities to meet the Master, you will still be the Master's disciple. The tree promised to do as told. He further vowed to imitate Guanyin Bodhisattva in making the resolve to universally save living beings in the future. Right then, I saw the tree turn into a monk, kneeling on the ground with hands folded, and Guanyin Bodhisattva appeared above him and anointed the crown of his head with pure water from a vase. I was deeply touched. I reported this matter to the Master after we got home. The Master took it seriously and asked me to get more details about the tree. His name is Ren Neng (Humane and Able). I asked him what his method of cultivation was. He said he has been reciting the *Heart Sutra* and investigating the principles in that Sutra. However, since he lacked the guidance of a good teacher, he had not fully understood it.

Since Upasika Yang is a sincere Buddhist who possesses the spiritual power to communicate with other species, the camphor tree made the request to take refuge with the Master through her. From now on the tree will receive guidance from a bright-eyed wise advisor. Upasika Yang asked the tree how he knew about the Master and why he wanted to take refuge with the Master. The tree said it was very simple: all living beings can hear the Master speaking Dharma. When the Master speaks the Dharma, all living beings throughout empty space and the Dharma Realm can see and hear the Master. However, people who are burdened by wealth, worldly things, fame, and desire for riches may look and listen, but they fail to see and hear. All other living beings are quietly cultivating, steeped in the sound of the Master's Dharma, nurturing their seeds of Bodhi. So the tree had been listening to the Master's Dharma for a long time.

That day at Long Beach Monastery, before the refuge ceremony ended, the Master made a special point of emphasizing the importance of cultivation. He said, whoever you are, if you have a true and sincere mind; if you are not careless in the least; if you do not do what worldly people do, but do the contrary, then you will be able to attain the benefit of Buddhism. So, monks and nuns and laypeople should all be true Buddhists; be different from ordinary people; don't be like ordinary people who fight, are greedy, who seek, who are selfish, who pursue self-benefit, and who lie, not letting a moment go by from morning to night without lying.

That is vitally important! These Six Principles are the first step toward learning Buddhism and to eventually realizing Buddhahood. Don't forget them! Don't neglect them! We should learn to take more losses and not take any advantages.

THE GOOD
AND WISE
ADVISOR'S
TEACHINGS
FOR ME

ଔ Shr Heng Sure

Many disciples experienced the Venerable Abbot's teachings in person and know the dynamic experience of drawing near a Good and Wise Advisor; many others did not, but knew the Master through his books or by reputation only. Scolding is perhaps the most misunderstood aspect of his teachings when viewed by those who did not understand its use among the many skillful expedient means of a true Wise Teacher.

At that time the Youth Good Wealth bowed at his feet, stood, put his palms together, and said, "Sagely One, I have already brought forth the resolve for Anuttarasamyaksambodhi, but I still do not know how a Bodhisattva studies the Bodhisattva Conduct and how he cultivates the Bodhisattva path. I heard that the Sagely One is skilled at guiding and teaching. I wish you would explain this for me."

The Brahman said, "Good Man, if you can now go up this mountain of knives and throw yourself into the mass of fire, then all your Bodhisattva conduct will be purified."

Chapter on Entering the Dharma Realm,

The *Flower Adornment Sutra*

Shr Fu taught in many skillful ways; one of the more dramatic was his "scoldings." I am one of several disciples who frequently got the benefit of Shr Fu's focused energy via the expedient of scoldings.

In the world, scolding is something universally feared; for that reason a tongue-lashing is effective as a means of discipline and behavior modification. It only works, however, if the one doing the scolding has personal virtue. If there is real anger behind the words, then scolding will produce hatred and anger in return.

We disciples knew that the thundering storm of anger was a technique, because the Abbot could be blasting away to correct a mistake by one disciple, and then in a twinkling turn his head to gently encourage another disciple in the crowd. In another eyeblink, he would return to the fault of the miscreant and send more lightning shafts towards him. These two modes of teaching—(1) subduing and humbling the arrogant and hard; and (2) enticing and embracing the timid and cautious—appear in Sutra descriptions of the Buddha's own two methods of teaching: hard and soft, turned on and off at will. Those who watched closely would see the compassionate, impassive, kindly teacher behind the heat.

In fact only the closest disciples got scolded harshly at all; and among them, it seemed that scolding came in a sense as a reward for hard work. We "earned" our scoldings. But this did not make them any easier to take.

I recall being scolded once on live television (Channel 5), at the San Francisco airport, and several times while translating on a lecture stage before thousands of people. In my memory, the worst scoldings came overseas: in Hong Kong, in Taiwan, in Calgary. No time was ever too public, too embarrassing to prevent a chance to teach a student who was ripe for a scolding. Sometimes those well-timed tongue-lashings marked an unexpected turning point in a disciple's life.

Once at Gold Mountain an error I made brought on a public reprimand that kept the entire assembly standing at their bowing benches for ninety minutes. The volume and the impact of the rebuke created distaste in some of the onlookers and listeners, but not in the recipient. Strangely enough, its effects, besides producing shame and a wish to change, were clear seeing, lightness, and calm, like the state at the eye of the tornado. Of course it helped to know about the proverbial Chinese father who "*pan zi cheng long*" "reprimands his children to turn them into dragons." That is, scolding strengthens one's bones. Most often the scolding produced a memorable opportunity to get priceless instructions.

For example, once I sent away an important guest by mistake, and got scolded so hard I thought I should run away, or perhaps die. I didn't die, and the next morning the Abbot frowned and asked me how I felt.

"I felt like I ought to die. I felt inadequate, useless, and forlorn. Maybe I *would* rather die," I said.

"You won't die. That would just be cheating. Dying would be easier than changing your bad habits. Where is your copy of the *Ultimate End of the Dharma Sutra*? Get it and read to me." I ran to my desk and found the requested text. I knelt in the Buddhahall in front of the Master. I read the story of the future day when Buddhism will completely disappear from the planet.

The Abbot sat with a distant gaze, keeping a half dozen disciples waiting, each of whom had urgent business—real estate, banking, international phone calls, and offerings—to settle, while he listened to my recitation of the text in clumsy Chinese.

As I read, I felt sweat break out on my face and body. My temperature rose and I felt faint, as if something were being purged and carried out of me. I kept reading and the sensation passed, leaving me lighter, cooler, and calmer. All traces of my earlier mood of self-pity were gone.

The Master exhorted in a stern voice, "You have left home to follow me, and now you are not like you were before; now you have to cultivate the Way; You are a disciple of the Buddha, you belong to the Buddha's family. Do you see how important your words and actions are? In this country you represent the Buddha, the Dharma, and the Sangha. Do you understand? You're not living just for yourself any longer. How can you be heedless and selfish? Don't you see the road you are on?" Great Master Yung Chia saw it.

Once I saw the road to Tsao Creek, I recognized the phenomenon of birth and death and had nothing further to do with them.

The Venerable Abbot continued: "You've got to try harder. A casual effort like before won't get you over the Dragon Gate. I've got high expectations for you. How can you just muddle through, like somebody who is simply eating his fill and waiting for death to catch up to him? Living like somebody born drunk and dying in a dream is good enough for others, but disciples of the Buddha have to be models for both humans and gods. You have to surpass the ordinary and excel the standards. You have to endure what others can't endure, eat food that others can't eat, take on suffering that others can't take on, and practice what others can't practice. You have to be patient where others cannot be patient. Only then will you pass the tests ahead. Take propagating the Dharma as your personal responsibility. Otherwise, Buddhism won't take root in this country."

Good Wealth said, "Strange indeed, Sagely One. When my body came into contact with this mountain of knives and great mass of fire, I felt peaceful, serene, and joyous.

Chapter on Entering the Dharma Realm,

The *Flower Adornment Sutra*

The scolding may have been the catalyst that jolted the memory of my past vows into awareness, because several days later I had the vision that led to my making the resolve to begin the "Three Steps, One Bow" pilgrimage for world peace. The Venerable Abbot observed that night after the Sutra lecture,

> All of you in the past have been together with Vairochana Buddha. We have been together investigating the Buddhadharma. And way back then I said we should all go to America and do it. Some of you made the vows of monks and some the vows of nuns. Some made the vows of Dharma-protectors. Others made the vows to be translators. Some of you made vows to build Way-places; and others to teach school.
>
> Now we are all here to fulfill our vows. From limitless kalpas past our causes and conditions with one another have been deep. They create a strength of togetherness that endures... And in the Hall of Ten Thousand Buddhas you can make vows, so in the future we can all become Ten Thousand Buddhas. Three-Steps-One-Bow are seeking Ten Thousand Buddhas to protect ten thousand peoples. In the midst of a dream, we are all here doing the Buddhas' work...

This phrase rings loudest in my mind recently among all the many instructions I've received from the Venerable Abbot in the last twenty years:

> Here we are, in the midst of a dream doing the work of the Buddhas.

I recall kneeling in the aisle of a bus on a sweltering sunny afternoon in Taoyuan, Taiwan, outside the gate of a monastery. The delegation from Dharma Realm Buddhist University was caught in a titanic traffic jam, caused by our visit to the Republic of China. The cars were coming to listen to the Venerable Abbot speak Dharma and transmit the precepts. People had gotten out of their cars to scratch their heads and to discuss the scene. I was kneeling in the aisle because the Venerable Abbot, to pass the time constructively, had asked the members of the delegation to stand up and give Dharma-talks. "Anywhere and anytime is a good place to cultivate the Way" was one of the Master's favorite travel maxims.

I had been receiving mighty scoldings since before we got on the plane in San Francisco, and I had been apprehensive day and night, fearing to do anything else wrong and anxious to escape the withering glare and lion's roar of the Good and Wise Advisor. The Master had called me out first and ordered me to speak Dharma. I felt exhausted and overwhelmed. The heat, the diarrhea, the pressure of my faults grinding against my teacher's will that I change for the Dharma, for the better, all put my head in a spin, and I couldn't utter a sound. I could only kneel there mute and limp.

"Kuo Chen!" said the Abbot, and suddenly I entered another zone, and as if transported in time I recalled a moment in Malibu on my bowing pilgrimage alongside the highway when the California Highway Patrol pulled up to tell us to be careful of the road ahead because it was narrow and fast. The officer was a slow-speaking, sun-browned cowboy with a twinkle in his eye. "You fellers had better stay way over on the shoulder, and tell that Chinese gentleman behind you to do the same. His red robe helps make him a bit more visible, but this is a fast road, and I don't want any accidents on my shift. Our CHP attorney called on his way to work, said he had spotted you and wanted us to make sure you get safely through Malibu. My wife saw you, too, and told me to remind the three of you to be careful. Take care, fellas." We thanked him, and, after he left, sheepishly looked behind us for the third member of our team, the "Chinese gentleman." We couldn't see anyone, let alone somebody in a red robe.

"Three monks, he said?"

"Strange. I wonder who they saw."

Only months later in San Francisco did a laywoman tell us the other side of the story. During that time of the pilgrimage, frequently in the mornings or afternoons the Venerable Abbot would be speaking with them and would suddenly stand up and walk into his room and shut the door. They would never know what he did inside, but usually after an hour or so, he would emerge and say, "They're all right now, *mei you shi qing,* it's okay." The CHP officers' request suggested that the Venerable Abbot's vows were helping him supervise the pilgrimage of two young monks from six hundred miles away. The Abbot's seventeenth vow says, "I vow in this life to attain the Five Eyes and Six Penetrations, and the ability to fly freely."

The image brought me back to the stifling bus in Taoyuan, and I believe the Venerable Abbot was observing my insight, because now he was smiling and his tone was gentle, instead of severe. "Kuo Chen here speaks from experience. You should listen to what he has to say, because he knows that without a Good and Wise Advisor he would probably be foundering in the Saha world's sea of suffering by now. Isn't that right, Kuo Chen? You were already full of bad habits when you came through the door of Gold Mountain Monastery, don't you remember? You might have sunk beneath the current of birth and death if it weren't for your affinities with a Good Advisor, right? Why don't you tell these people about it?"

I nodded in agreement and looked at my teacher. That week in Taiwan he was not eating any solid food because he was fasting and dedicating the merit to Taiwan and her people, hoping to delay the disaster that pundits were predicting. He was sick as well, which only the monks who attended him were aware of. Once the bus arrived, he would be surrounded by clouds of disciples and seekers, each of whom brought his special request for healing, for a blessing, for help, seeking the Master's powers and abilities.

Often in Taiwan he wouldn't sleep for days, choosing instead to stay up and talk with the line of seekers outside his door, which did not diminish day and night. They came hoping for a chance to draw near and make their request, and to be touched by his compassion.

None of us disciples could stand in for him or pick up even a finger's worth of his burden. Yet he feared no toil or pain. He existed only to dispense the teachings of sweet dew. The teaching of the Great Good and Wise Advisor relieves the suffering of living beings. I opened my mouth and spoke the following lines from the *Avatamsaka Sutra* that I had memorized long ago on a hot Sunday afternoon on a highway outside San Luis Obispo:

> The Youth Good Wealth contemplated and reflected upon the instructions of his Good and Wise Advisor: He was like the great sea, which receives the rains from the great clouds without satiation. He had the following thought:
>
> The Good and Wise Advisor's teaching is like a spring sun in that it produces and makes grow the roots and sprouts of all good Dharmas;
>
> The Good and Wise Advisor's teaching is like a full moon, in that it refreshes and cools everything it shines on;
>
> The Good and Wise Advisor's teaching is like a snow mountain in summer, in that it can dispel the heat and thirst of all beasts;
>
> The Good and Wise Advisor's teaching is like the sun on a fragrant pool, in that it can open the lotus flower

of the mind of all goodness;

The Good and Wise Advisor's teaching is like a great jeweled continent, in that the various Dharma jewels fill his heart;

The Good and Wise Advisor's teaching is like the Jambu tree, in that it amasses the flowers and fruits of all blessings and wisdom;

The Good and Wise Advisor's teaching is like a great dragon king, in that he playfully roams with ease and comfort in empty space;

The Good and Wise Advisor's teaching is like Mt. Sumeru, in that limitless wholesome dharmas of the Heaven of the Thirty-three are situated in its midst;

The Good and Wise Advisor's teaching is like Lord Shakra, who is circumambulated by his multitudes and assemblies, in that none can overshadow him, and who can subdue bizarre cults and hosts of Asura armies. In this way he reflected.

I brought the verses out from my memory effortlessly, I was too tired to think up any doubts or my usual discursive thoughts. The Venerable Abbot seemed very happy, as with a broad grin he said, "See? Everything I teach you has its function and its purpose. Now do you understand?"

As the bus started to roll on up the hill, he said, "Who else wants to speak the Dharma? Don't be lazy. These people have spared no expense to bring you all the way here from America. Can you just eat your fill and wait to die? You owe them some teachings to repay their kindness. Who will be the next Wise Advisor? Don't wait for me to spoon-feed you all your life. All right, who will it be? Step up here. Next!"

HOW
MY ENTIRE
LIFE
WAS
CHANGED!

ೞ Shr Heng Tso

I first met the Venerable Master in December of 1967 when I was eighteen years old. At that time he was living in a temple occupying the fourth floor at Waverly Place, in San Francisco's Chinatown. The background for my first meeting with the Venerable Master goes as follows:

Upon graduation from high school, Steve Mechling, my good friend at the time, and I traveled together first to Mexico and then Hawaii. While living in Hawaii, Steve corresponded with his eldest brother, Nick Mechling, who was living on Sutter Street in the same building as the Venerable Master. Steve told me that Nick would go listen to the Venerable Master lecture on the Sutras every week and would also mention various things about the Venerable Master in his letters. Because I was living the life of a carefree surfer, I didn't really have much interest in what Steve told me. However, after a very profound religious experience in the dormant volcano, Haleakala, on the island of Maui, I became very interested in spiritual pursuits and wished to find a teacher who could explain such things. I enjoyed living the surfing life, but the pressures of possibly being drafted to fight in Vietnam and the profound religious experience I had just gone through forced me to take my existence more seriously.

Around Christmas time, Steve and I left Hawaii to return to California where we planned to enroll in college and settle down. [Editor's note: During the Vietnam War, high school graduates in the United States could avoid the draft by enrolling in college.] Following Steve's suggestion we decided to first go to San Francisco to visit his brother before returning to our homes in Los Angeles. Little did I know how much this decision would change my entire life.

When we arrived in San Francisco, it was already dark and very cold. We didn't know anything about the city. With suitcases and sleeping bags in tow, we took two buses to get to Nick and his wife Susan's house. We were quite excited and talked late into the night. One plan we made was to go soon to the Buddhist Lecture Hall to meditate and hear the Master lecture.

At that time the Master was lecturing on Monday and Wednesday evenings and also on Sunday afternoons. The evening lectures, scheduled from eight to nine o'clock, were preceded by one hour of meditation. Those who attended were mostly young Americans. Because the Master lectured in Mandarin Chinese, a couple of boys in their late teens, Kim Lee and Jimmy Wong, were always present to translate.

The first lecture we attended was in the evening. I remember climbing the three long flights of very squeaky stairs to the Buddhist Lecture Hall and entering to find a few people seated on bowing cushions facing the walls. There was a strong smell of Chinese incense and the room was dimly lit. After meditating for most of an hour, someone rang a small handbell and more lights were turned on. A few more people had come during the meditation period and now there were about fifteen people present. The Master sat at the head of a long table formed of four small tables pushed together and proceeded to give a very animated lecture. I don't remember a single word he said. In fact I didn't have much of a feeling for him or Buddhism at the time. I arrogantly thought to myself that enlightenment is a serious business, but the Master's lecture didn't seem to confirm my feelings.

After we returned to Nick and Susan's house, we talked about the evening's experience. I asked Nick if it was possible to go and talk with the Master. I wanted to discuss my volcano experience with him. Both Nick and Susan, to my surprise, encouraged me to call him. So, the next day I called and asked the Master if I could come for a visit. His response was very warm and encouraging, and he asked me to come the next evening.

The next evening, when Steve and I reached the temple, we timidly pushed the door open. It was dimly lit as before. The Master was sitting on a bowing cushion facing the door and motioned for us to come over to him. Then he directed us to each get a bowing cushion and sit down on either side of him. The first thing he asked was if we could sit in full lotus position. I said I could because I had started practicing about a month earlier. The Master looked at my legs and said I was sitting with the wrong leg on top and that I should reverse them. I did this with a little more difficulty, and then we proceeded to talk about all kinds of things.

Because we didn't know any Chinese and couldn't understand the Master's English very well, we had some difficulty communicating at first. However, the Master has many ways to communicate, and it didn't take long for us to become totally enthralled with what he was saying and doing.

At one point, the Master took my left hand and put it next to his left hand. Then he used his right hand to point out the similar lines on the palms of our hands. Right then something clicked inside, and I knew what he was saying. Because my entire life to that point had been so foreign to that of a monk's lifestyle, I didn't know how I could ever conduct myself in the proper manner, but still I found myself asking the Master if I could be a monk. The Master replied that becoming a monk was a lifetime commitment and not to be taken lightly. After some more discussion, the Master said I could leave home if I got my parents' permission.

Towards the end of our conversation, the Master said I could take a translation of the *Sixth Patriarch Sutra* from a shelf to my right and borrow it to read. Forgetting that I had been sitting in full lotus, I stood up abruptly and fell down just as fast. In the past I had been able to keep my legs up for just a few minutes at most. Because I was so concentrated this time, I had completely forgotten about the pain in my legs and didn't even realize that they had gone numb. Fortunately I didn't hurt myself.

After a week, Steve and I hitchhiked south to our homes. When we mentioned our plan to become monks to our parents, there was a lot of concern in both households. Steve's mother convinced him that he should wait a bit, and my parents wanted me to go see their local pastor and a psychologist. I complied with their wish and after numerous conversations, agreed to wait until I graduated from college before becoming a monk. I think all of us were relieved with this decision.

After the Christmas holidays, Steve and I drove my Volkswagen bug back to San Francisco to live and study with the Master. When we told him of our decision not to leave the home-life right away, he suggested that we enroll in college. We checked into City College of San Francisco but found that registration was already closed. At someone's suggestion, we enrolled at College of Marin, north of the Golden Gate Bridge, rented a small house nearby, and began our studies in a couple of weeks. This was the beginning of a long relationship that continues to this day. What follows are many experiences and teachings the Master has provided.

Many things happened during the winter and spring of 1968. Many people drew near the Master and were taught by him. Janice Vickers Storss (Gwo Jin) came from Texas, and Nancy Lovett, Steven Lovett's (Heng Gwan) wife, returned to the United States from Taiwan. Spring break also brought a few students from the University of Washington including Ron Epstein, Jon Babcock, Steve Klarer, Randy and Theresa Dinwiddie, and Loni Baur (Gwo Yi), who came to the Buddhist Lecture Hall to attend a meditation session. Because our spring break did not coincide with the others', Steve and I could only attend for the weekend. However, even just two days of meditation made us feel extremely happy.

Besides the Master's lectures on Monday and Wednesday evenings, Joe Miller also lectured on Tuesday evenings. Because we were full-time students living thirty miles away from San Francisco, Steve and I could not attend all the lectures. When we could, we would go into the city around four or five o'clock to visit with the Master and others for a while before the evening meditation and lecture. This was a very good chance to investigate many basic questions. One time the Master asked me about my girlfriends. He said sex should wait until marriage. During the late 1960s, the sexual revolution had changed everyone's thinking, and this was not something I expected to hear. That was my first glimpse of the real teachings of Buddhism.

One afternoon Janice Vickers Storss and Nancy Lovett told us they were going to take refuge. That afternoon the Master asked Steve if he was interested, and I requested to be included as well. The Master consented and set a date. On February 7, 1968, just three days before my nineteenth birthday, the four of us took refuge with the Master and formally became disciples of the Triple Jewel. The ceremony lasted for about an hour, and the Master did his own translation.

In the spring of 1968, my parents came to visit us and to see who this person was who had caused me to change so much. As was the case when anyone's parents come, the Master was happy to meet them. Unfortunately, on the afternoon of their visit, the only one there to translate was Alice Lum, one of the Master's disciples from Hong Kong whose English was not very good. During the conversation she got quite flustered. My mother, who can be very direct, asked the Master, "What are your credentials, and where are you from?" The Master replied that she should ask me, her son. My mother wanted to get to the bottom of things, and she thought the direct route was the correct way to deal with the situation. Unfortunately, Alice couldn't cope, but just when it looked like we had reached an impasse, Joe Miller and his wife walked in the door. Joe, a white-haired man with a goatee and a vaudeville past, proceeded to explain Buddhism in his own dramatic self-styled way. When the conversation ended, my mother was quite turned around and left with a satisfied feeling. However, my father was still somewhat suspicious.

Sometime during the spring, the Master announced that there would be a Shurangama Sutra summer study session held at the Buddhist Lecture Hall. It would last all summer and single men could stay in the temple and others could stay at another house or on Pine Street. Immediately after school was out, Steve and I went home for a short visit and then went back to the temple to attend the session.

During the session, the meals were taken care of by two people each week. Everyone also took turns washing dishes and cleaning up. Three meals were served each day, but as the Master encouraged us to eat a vegetarian diet and take one meal a day, more and more people began to skip dinner and breakfast. The Master also urged us to stop bad habits like smoking cigarettes and other substances. By the end of the summer, many of us had begun following his instructions, and when it came time to take the precepts, those with long hair and beards cut their hair and shaved off their beards. Many of the women also cut their hair shorter.

At the beginning, Kim Lee translated the evening lecture, but after a week or so, those attending the session full time began to translate for all the lectures. The translators were Ron Epstein, Paul Hansen, Jon Babcock, Steve Klarer, and Julie Plant. They all took turns and spent a lot of time preparing before each lecture. At that time, I wasn't aware of any internal conflicts. One day, however, none of the translators showed up and the Master had to translate for himself. The tapes for the afternoon lecture on the 4th of July are testimony to this.

After the summer session, Steve and I went back to school at College of Marin. An estate within walking distance of the school was looking for a caretaker, and I was tempted to move there, but when I discussed it with the Master, his reply stopped me cold in my tracks. He said, "If you move from here, you will not come back." Therefore, I decided to remain living at the Buddhist Lecture Hall and commute to school.

The Venerable Master devoted his time to many different things, and everything he did was to benefit living beings. I remember going with him to the park to feed hungry birds.

In the mid 1970s California suffered through a severe drought. During those years, I sometimes had the opportunity to drive the Venerable Master to different places in the San Francisco Bay Area. One particular day, my three year old daughter and I (I was still married at the time) came to pick him up early in the morning. After he climbed into the car, the Master asked me if I knew of any lakes in Golden Gate Park. I said I knew of a few, and he said, "Let's go take a look." After showing him three or four, he selected one smaller lake that was a bit more secluded than the others we had seen. As we got out of the car, from the canvas shopping bag he often took with him when he went out, he pulled a plastic bag full of left-over bread and said, "We are going to feed the birds."

Walking over to a bench and sitting down, he instructed us to recite the Great Compassion Mantra as we fed the birds. In no time we were surrounded by hundreds of birds including different kinds of gulls, loons, and ducks. they flew all around us grabbing the bread as we threw it in the air. Sometimes they landed on our shoulders as they fought to get closer to the food source. We must have looked like three flowers being swarmed by a hive of bees. A couple of gulls were the most aggressive, and the Master teased them by tossing bread in the opposite direction. Then all three of us would laugh at their foiled attempts to steal the bread from the other birds. This feeding went on for about twenty minutes until the bread ran out. After the last crumb was eaten, we got up to leave and the Venerable Master said, "They are very hungry." I reasoned it was probably a result of the drought. The very next day we did the same thing.

The Master didn't just lecture Dharma. He taught by doing, and his classroom was the Dharma Realm. Although he was lecturing the *Avatamsaka Sutra* eight times per week, establishing new monasteries, helping numerous people with their problems, and probably doing a lot of other things we weren't aware of, he still took time to feed birds that were suffering from the results of a drought. For him no matter was too small to tend to, and no matter was too big. His only wish was that we learn to be that way too.

One final observation: The way the birds acted with the Master was quite extraordinary. They were all over us seeking a handout. I didn't realize how unusual their behavior was until about two years later, when I returned to the same pond to again feed the birds. I expected them to swarm around me as they had done before, but this time only a few birds appeared, and they kept their distance.

THE MASTER'S LITERARY WORKS CONVEY THE TRUTH

Cȣ   Shr Heng Sure

Many people have sat here in the last few days, and will continue to do so, talking about their memories of their teacher, talking about the Master's contributions to education, to translation and Sutra lecturing, propagating the Dharma, creating the Sangha, making Way-places, and so on. Everyone has said what was on their heart, and we have many more to hear later today. But I wanted to share something that I think is rare.

Probably not many people today, if they were asked what was the Venerable Master's outstanding feature, would say, "The Master was a poet without peer. He was a literati, a writer, an editor, a social commentator, and a historian without peer." And yet the Venerable Master wrote an eight-line verse for every line of the Great Compassion Mantra and every line of the Shurangama Mantra. He wrote the Verses without a Stand for the *Heart Sutra*. He wrote verses for the Patriarchs, adding to Elder Master Hsu Yun's *Lives of the Patriarchs*. He wrote not only verses but excellent rhymed essays. He was a master of prose and verse. The Master's scattered writings, occasional verses, and songs number in the hundreds. One of the things about the Master that has touched me the most is his contribution to literature, in the form of songs, essays, and poetry.

The Master would teach a matching couplets class, in which he would put the first line on the board regarding a state or a situation or a disciple's habits, and invite everyone else to come up and add the second line. It was amazing how just the few Chinese characters of your couplet line could reveal your character, your nature, your shortcomings, your literary skill, your education... He even had children who were not able to speak Chinese come up and put matching couplets on the board that were surprisingly sophisticated in form and refreshingly pure and straight in content. It was a wonderful experience to have the Master teach couplets. It's probably the first time in any American Way-place that a Buddhist teacher has done this (and maybe the first time in Chinese Buddhist history for a long time). So this is just to point to one aspect of our teacher that I think needs to be remembered.

What kind of a poet was he? I'd like to tell a very personal story, because it shows the way the Master taught. Perhaps many people who talked today never actually got a teaching from the Abbot, and they don't what it was really like to be on the receiving end of his teaching—how bittersweet that experience could be. So I'd like to talk about how the Abbot taught me and caught my mind in a place where I didn't even know I was vulnerable. This was on a bowing pilgrimage I did with another monk. We got to a place called Half Moon Bay on the coast. I was bowing along when something inspired me and I wrote down a poem. I thought, "That's a pretty good poem. Boy, I can write Chinese poetry! This really has captured my state. I'm going to give it to the Master next time I see him." We hadn't seen the Master for about three weeks. When you're cultivating alone, it's really easy to get into a state and think you're hot stuff. My poem went like this:

> *Words are false; books are many.*
> *Energy is precious, and Buddhas are few.*
> *Still dreaming? Stop talking.*
> *Do no more false thinking.*
> *After awakening, cross living beings over in everything you do.*

Pretty good poem, huh? I was working on it—which is called false thinking—I should have been bowing, not thinking about what a great poet I was. I thought, "Well, someday I'll have a chance to read it to the Master." At lunchtime, a familiar station wagon pulled off the road; it was the Master and some other people. After the meal, I cleared my throat and said, "Master, I wrote a poem! Could I read it to you?" He said, "Hmpf! *You* wrote a poem? All right, let's hear it." So I said my poem. He said, "Not bad. But I want to change it." He said,

> *Your words are false, your excuses are many.*
> *Value your energy, and you can become a Buddha.*
> *You're still dreaming? Really stop talking,*
>   *and do no more false thinking.*
> *After awakening, you'll see all along that there hasn't been*
>   *a single word in it anywhere.*

Right on the spot! It took him less than a minute. He turned my own words around and pointed right at my false thinking. My wonderful poem was scattered to the wind. He made it not only a better poem, but exactly the right teaching for my mind. It was like looking in a mirror. Here I'd been, very proud of myself, and in the blink of an eye, the Master showed me—"See? False thinking. Go back to work." So this is the Master—the poet, the literati, and the teacher.

WHAT DID THE VENERABLE MASTER TEACH US?

ଔ   Snjezana Akpinar

In asking "What did the Venerable Master Hua teach?" one seems to step into shoes which are more than several sizes too large. It is not easy to answer that question, no matter which way we try to address it. That is probably why I decided to start from a beginning which is very personal. I see it as part of my attempt to understand Buddhism and explain it when the need arises. The most obvious part of the Master's teaching, in my view, is the attitude of East towards West and vice versa. The Venerable Master showed us how to cultivate an ability to spot well ingrained stereotypes which our own cultures and civilizations carry within them and impose on us from a very early age. When speaking within the sphere of education, particularly when children are involved, that should not be so hard to achieve.

For Westerners one of the cures could be stories from distant lands, be they India, China, or Japan, as well as stories written by those who went to such distant places and wrote about them when they returned. For Easterners the cure, I presume, would lie in the opposite approach, stories about the West. One must never lose track, however, no matter how nice distant tales may be, that there are also those who see it all here and now, and are capable of illustrating the obvious by telling children and grown-ups stories about our immediate surroundings. But, it is still up to each one of us to continue in the same vein and find the inner courage to go beyond a particular point of view.

At first I thought that I should not write anything on such complicated subjects, that what the Venerable Master has taught is beyond words, so why keep on talking and telling others what to do? It is not my place. There are enough eloquent people around, and it is always the same. I do not wish and cannot be a judge in instances like these. The Venerable Master's influence changed a whole generation of Westerners and Easterners, both here in the New World and in the Old one. I always felt somewhat awkward when asked to speak, anyway. Whenever invited to sit next to the Venerable Master I was sure that hidden within the invitation there was a sincere wish to help me, and that the university and all other educational endeavors were only secondary. Actually I never seriously discussed all this, it was easier to go along to the best of my capacities, and it is impossible to resist such sincere wishes.

So after all of this I would like to explain that here I do not intend to analyze the Venerable Master's intentions, nor my own, since I am very incapable to do that, I never approached such sublime heights. Nevertheless, even without trying very hard it is not that impossible to spot the different points of view among all of his disciples. It is out of such ambiguities that I decided to write a few words and in this manner return to some of my own feelings and thoughts about the whole issue of education. I may be able to draw some conclusions not only about the Master's vision of a university, but also about the current activities in the fields of Buddhist studies in particular and religious studies in general, things I somehow stumble upon in spite of myself.

All of us who have been around Buddhism and the Venerable Master long enough learned to approach cliches and pre-packaged ideas with great caution. This goes for the whole spectrum, from the simplest to the most complex of thoughts. I believe that most of us have learned to steer away from prejudices, to spot them. This attitude in itself should be enough of a guide through anyone's life. It gives a general and freeing direction, an open door. But, as in anything that concerns our world, the next step is also very important. One could approach it in the following manner: Fine, we are now free, the door is open, but now what? What are we to do with our knowledge, and will we have enough strength to withstand? How far away from the open door do we dare to go? Some of us have natures that are more energetic and temperamental and are steadily pushed into battle for the sake of righteousness in an immediate manner full of indignation. Such people do not allow themselves to skirt political issues and "engagement" with the world and its struggles. Actually the word "engaged" is probably not well chosen here, but I cannot think of a better way to word this whole aspect of our nature. It is my private attempt to explain something complex in an easy way.

This country is full of such vigorous and "engaged" attitudes. I also am often attracted to such thoughts, mostly because of a sense of indignation felt by most of those who want the world to be a better place. But, if viewed from the point of view of the Venerable Master, at least as I perceive it, it is exactly these feelings which create the stumbling stones that we should avoid. Or, to word it in a better way, we should be aware of the existence of such stumbling stones and behave more cautiously exactly because they happen to be on our path. These obstacles should be viewed, if possible, from a healthy distance in order to grasp their totality through very broad perspective and at any given moment. That seems to be the only way a human being may be able to untangle himself from the "thicket of views" and the "jungle of views" as the Blessed Buddha had said, with a minimum of bruises and consequences to ourselves and our surroundings.

Only then may we hope to reach a somewhat higher, clearer plateau. I am not a psychologist and I cannot explain all of this. Even this much is already too much, I fear. I can only quote, off the top of my head, as a further illustration of the same point, a letter which my father once long ago wrote to his brother and the rest of his family explaining why he decided to become a monk (my uncle at the time was horrified):

> There are some very refined and subtle reasons, very hard to perceive and even harder to understand unless you live a certain kind of life and have some sort of talent for the contemplative life. By this I mean a capacity to slow your thoughts down so that the sheer strength of the stream does not carry you away and throw you against some rock.

In these last years, since having lived at the City of Ten Thousand Buddhas, I began to glimpse the contours of that answer. What helped me most, was the steady onslaught of the "engaged" Buddhists, Islamists and others who very energetically mill around Berkeley and occasionally visit the City of Ten Thousand Buddhas. Many of the inhabitants of the City in the face of such attitudes patiently carried on with their cultivation. I tried to protect and criticize both, and somehow convinced myself that the Venerable Master put up with me in the hopes that I will derive some better degree of clarity from the whole issue.

The life of the Venerable Master remains a true example of how we can live in the truth, as Gandhi once had said. It is a way of life which helps us let go of our tight grips and our wishes to hold on to the our various "views" and points of view. It is Buddhism itself, and it can also be defined as a religious approach in the true sense of that word—an approach which stems from a certain foreknowledge, an awareness, based (for want of better words) on a co-feeling, an empathy, toward all living beings, a sort of filter built into, hopefully, the majority of living beings. I often imagine it as a primordial sieve, all of us should try and clean every once in a while. The action of cleansing is exactly that superhuman effort which demands that we be constantly aware, awake, and watchful. All religions are, in their essence, systems and methods which teach us how to do this more effectively. The effort and insight gained by such efforts should help us surpass all the "isms" and biases and multitudes of words. There are simply no words, they do not exist, which could describe all of these things.

As good Buddhists we also need to cultivate an awareness of the process of disintegration: from the withering of leaves falling around us to the greater and more striking phenomena. It is a process which at first strikes us as being frightening, but after a while we may also get the feeling that the death of a human being is one last educational tool, usually employed by parents to teach their children how to grow up. None of us, no matter how hard we may try to avoid such a lesson, is ever capable of escaping it.

A FIRSTHAND
EXPERIENCE WITH
FIRE-BREATHING
DOGS

ભ   Terri Nicholson

My husband Alan and I have been disciples of the Venerable Master for over 25 years. This particular incident occurred in 1985 when our daughter, Marcelle, had just turned three years old. She has lived her entire life at the City of Ten Thousand Buddhas and took refuge with the Master at four months of age. Before she was born, the Master named her Wonderful Flower.

At the end of the summer of 1985 our family went to Mount Lassen National Park to spend some time with Alan's brother. Mount Lassen is an inactive volcano which last errupted in 1916. There are, however, still steaming pits and boiling mud in the park as well as caves created by the last volcano eruptions. Americans consider it a fascinating and unusual place to visit and are completely unaware that it is dangerous in any way. Unfortunately, at the time, my husband and I were equally ignorant.

From the time we arrived at the park we felt uncomfortable, mainly because a great deal of hunting and fishing was going on. At the lodge where we originally planned to stay, there was a pond where you could pick your own fish for lunch and penned deer whose mothers had been hunted and killed. Because we felt so uncomfortable, we decided to stay outside of the park. Marcelle was particularly ill at ease and asked several

81

times to go home to see the Master and hear the Sutra lecture. Since we'd already made plans with Alan's brother, we stayed anyway. The rest of the week was uneventful except for a trip into one of the caves in the park where Marcelle became extremely frightened and upset.

For several months after we returned home, Marcelle complained of nightmares of wolves chasing and biting her. We encouraged her to recite Guanyin's name, but, at the time, did not realize how serious the problem was. In the beginning of January, soon after her fourth birthday, Marcelle woke up early one morning screaming in pain and saying that her legs hurt. Later that day she seemed fine, but the leg pain continued. After a few days we took her to the doctor, who assumed it was some sort of virus. As her symptoms grew more painful and severe, we became increasingly alarmed. The pain became so severe that she was unable to sit up or walk. We planned to meet the doctor at the hospital but as we were getting ready to go, Marcelle began to insist that she wanted Shifu (the Master). The assembly was eating lunch with the Master and so we stopped to see him on the way to the hospital. Strangely, though Marcelle had asked to see him, as soon as we drew near she cried that she wanted to leave. The Master told us, "A karmic obstacle has come." When we explained that we were on our way to see the doctor, the Master replied, "They won't find anything." And they didn't. Blood tests were done and two doctors, a pediatrician and an orthopedist, examined her and could find nothing. They finally diagnosed it as a viral inflamation of the joints, but Marcelle was not in pain while we were there.

That afternoon we received a call from the office of the City of Ten Thousand Buddhas explaining that some sort of being had attached itself to Marcelle and was making her ill. We were instructed to recite Guanyin's name and the Great Compassion Mantra. However, Marcelle's condition worsened and she was in a great deal of pain. Normally a sweet-child, she developed a vicious temper and refused to cooperate in reciting at all. The only thing that calmed her was listening to a tape of the Master reciting Earth Treasury Bodhisattva's name.

Meanwhile the Master had gone to Vancouver. We became so alarmed at her worsening condition that we called there and asked for advice. The Master sternly exhorted us to recite more sincerely. He also said that Marcelle absolutely must not lose her temper and must recite Guanyin's name. With the help of friends we thought up every expedient device we could to help her. We gave her prizes for reciting, made books with her about getting better by reciting Guanyin's name and star charts to help her not get angry. She insisted that we add "not growling" to the chart, which later gained more significance. When the Master returned to the City, he came directly to our house to see Marcelle. After a long time he explained that volcanos are manifestations of hell on earth and that many hell-beings dwell there. (He first asked where we had taken her recently.) Residing at Mount Lassen was a fire-breathing dog and his retinue. These dogs are born inside the mountain in the lava and thrive on fire and anger. They have extremely cantankerous natures. When we visited Mt. Lassen, the leader was attracted to Marcelle's purity as a young disciple of the Master, and wished to make her part of his retinue. (This involved making her sick by biting her so that she was near death.) The Master said he'd convinced the leader to let her go, but that others in the retinue hadn't all agreed, so we had to continue to recite diligently. I cannot describe the pain we felt when we realized that we had "led her into the lion's den" and brought all this suffering upon her and trouble to the Master in our ignorance. We continued to recite and bow the Great Compassion Repentance and very gradually Marcelle's pain began to lessen and she was able to recite more. She would wake up screaming in pain, but if we could get her to recite Guanyin's name even for a few minutes she would fall into a more peaceful sleep.

I was moved also by Marcelle's young friends who lived at the City and who came each day to see her. Each gave her a gift of something they held precious and stayed to play by her bedside so she wouldn't be alone. They would also sit and recite Guanyin's name and try to get her to recite as well. Soon the pain went away completely and she was able to sit up and move around, though she was still unable to walk. The Master told us not to worry, that she would walk eventually.

Soon afterwards, Alan and I made a meal offering to the Sangha. At the beginning of the meal offering ceremony, Marcelle could walk only very awkwardly, but by the end of the meal she was walking around and playing with her friends. In the next few months Marcelle came down with an extremely high fever several times and I became frightened that she would get sick again. The Master compassionately explained that, yes, she had bumped into the fire-breathing dog again but that I shouldn't worry. If she got sick again he would help her get well. And so the three of us are eternally indebted to the Master for his great compassion not only in allowing us to bring up our child in this pure Way-place, but also in rescuing her from the jaws of death.

IN MEMORIAM WITH DEEPEST RESPECT

Shr Guo Xiu

The Buddhist Lecture Hall locale
In San Francisco's Chinatown
Was the Way-place where we awakened
To the wisdom of Foremost Shurangama,
To karma, to causes, effects, and more.

We found our Teacher who taught us before.
We wept for joy at this rare reunion.
If asked why we cried, no words came forth.
When we asked why, the answer was kind:
"You ride on vows you should renew."

"Take refuge with three—the Triple Jewel
And follow the precepts to make yourselves pure.
Precepts are the basis of Buddhism.
From them comes samadhi and then comes wisdom.
No outflows is the ultimate aim."

Directly he gave us Compassionate Dharmas
"I went high and low collecting these hands!
Say them every single day.
Turn them in; guard your light.
Be mindful of Guan Yin Bodhisattva!"

By the end of summer through study and practice
The shimmering goal: Shurangama Samadhi
Shone strong and ultimately firm.
A concentration beyond both entry and exit
Devoid of lust; defying death.

But our bodies—our weak and fickle flesh—
Were not so easily tamed by Truth.
And so the Abbot turned to Vajra
Prajna Paramita—the Middle Way.
To destroy our compulsive prejudiced views.

Tossing in the sea of suffering and sorrow.
We were told to bear what cannot be borne.
We were told to repent and advised to reform.
Sorry we were for our many mistakes.
Our minds became purer as offenses were purged.

The Standless Verses revealed the Heart.
The yellow child jumping; white billows ballooning.
Better than any Song yet sung.
When will these black waves cease?
How carefully our innocense must be kept!

Turning the wonderful Dharma wheel,
The Abbot never grew tired of teaching.
Bringing us Earth Store Bodhisattva,
He came on foot to our Laywomen's Forest
To proclaim the Sutra of Filial Piety.

Such mighty vows! Such gentle guidance!
How can we hope to repay that kindness?
"Only when no one is here in the hells
Will I consider my job complete."
A thump of his staff! A tinkle of rings!

Who was he, our Humble and Wise Advisor?
Some say he was indeed Earth Store.

Others say he was Cao Xi? Source.
Let me quote once upon a time:
"Who is Amitabha? I am Amitabha!"

Never mind, he would only deny it!
And say that to seek him in sound or sight
Is to miss by a thousand miles or more.
Was he not as is water when cut by a knife?
Could we compare him to blowing on light?

Unwearied, unworried he roamed at ease.
Bringing us word in this turbid world
Of a pure and pristine Buddha nature
Inherent in each and every being.
Exquisite like the Lotus supreme!

His relentless compassion never laxed.
"Time is like gold; but try to buy it!"
He urged us on to do our best
Only by his own example.
Remembering makes my conscience hurt.

The City of Ten Thousand Buddhas
Truly a Supreme and Holy Site!
He bore a debt so deep and heavy
It frightened the worldly; they ran away.
He remained unabashed at being abandoned.

Magnificient he stood; reminiscent of Sage-kings.
No one at all knew his sound.
Away from his land, in life-time exile,
He never betrayed his own country.
The Dharma Realm is his home.

Down into the dark, rich soil
Of this vast and vibrant Western land
He planted a small Bodhi seed.
First guiding its slender sprout with care,
Eventually he nurtured a tender trunk.

No task was too small for him to see through.
No blessing too great to give away.
All that he did for each of us,
Forgotten by him, is alive in our hearts!
To follow his Way is one tribute we pay.

But to follow the guidelines he stated so simply:
No fighting, no greed, no seeking, or selfishness;
Not searching for things that will bring me benefit
And never telling deliberate lies—
How hard I must try to embody these!

Unfolding the layer on layer of hosts
And attendants who serve those roles in turn,
He expounded the perfect Flower Adornment.
In dust motes are Buddhas; in hair-pores are lands—
Reciprocal, fused, and interconnected.

In that infinite microcosm of oneness
At last we found out who he was!
He was every Bodhisattva who ever
Gave away his eyes, his ears,
His heart, his health, his body and life.

For whom? For those who asked;
Or who listened but never heard the words.
For all of us who still have greed.
We took, he gave—his blood and breath.
Too late we wish he had suffered less.

Like the moon in waters his transformations abound.
In dreams he offers comforts and cures.
May we meet him again in Amita's pure land.
Meanwhile, we know what we must do:
Bring our own Bodhi resolve to perfection!

MY WISH
IS TO
TAKE ON THE
SUFFERINGS OF
LIVING BEINGS

ଔ   Stella Tan

The Venerable Master has employed all manner of means to teach stubborn living beings. All these years he has exhausted himself mentally and physically and eventually become sick. In order to gather all the gathas written by our Venerable Master, I reviewed my diary and unexpectedly found the following paragraphs spoken by the Venerable Master over three years ago. They reveal the great determination and willpower of the Venerable Master, so we decide to include them here.

Sunday, November 17, 1991

The Master said, "My wish is to take on the sufferings of living beings. I will suffer for the sake of living beings, especially in the last few years. I have a lot of offense karma, though it's gone now. Even offenses that fill up the sky will dissolve with one act of repentance." "Master, why do you say you've a lot of offense karma?" I asked in a puzzlement. "I scold people all the time. I take up the offense karma of living beings and place it in my physical self. I've been scolding good people, and not the bad."

Before, some disciples did not know why they got punished or scolded, and they could not accept it. (The Venerable Master treats left-home disciples and lay disciples the same way.) Now that you've read the above passage, you shall understand that the Venerable Master actually has done you a favor. Realizing the difficulty of saving living beings, the Venerable Master expressed concern in the following two gathas:

The Difficulty of Saving Living Beings

Written by the Venerable Master on the night of August 1, 1958.

Getting up early and retiring late,
Whom am I busy for?
Living beings are hard to ferry over,
How sad it is!

Fallen into this world of earthly dusts,
Their self-natures are upside-down.
Constant reminders are of no avail,
No other way I can employ.

The Grandeur of a Dream

What's there to admire in the grandeur of a dream,
Since the wealth and honor in front of your eyes are not real?
Why is it that fools are so attracted to them?
What a pity that they live drunk and die dreaming!

BLACK LINES ON WHITE PAPER

ଔ   Shi Guo Shan

Written words are simply black lines on white paper. Every syllable and phrase the Master uttered was sublime Truth. In an upside-down world of confusion and deceit, he dared to utter the Lion's great roar and dispel the darkness of ignorance. No human hero that ever existed could match him.

Not only did the Master expound on Sutras, he brought them to life before our very eyes. Anyone who's studied the Dharma knows that that is not a simple thing! To unlearned people, he made the most profound doctrine accessible. For the learned, he displayed the moon and exposed the finger as secondary.

There was no tiny act of kindness he would not take time to do. How he managed to do that, with such ease and grace, while the greatest troubles of the world sat on his shoulders, is in itself incredible. Not a single breath or thought of his contained even a particle, a wisp, of selfishness. He lived and breathed not only for the sake of rescuing living beings from suffering—that was not enough—but for the sake of teaching and transforming them; and in doing so he will never rest until all the living beings who have seen his face and heard his voice are brought to Bodhi. Anyone who has not yet had the good fortune to do so need not despair, but simply make the vow to see and hear him. If your heart is true, there is no doubt your wish will be fulfilled. The Master's vows are not just talk; they are not just black lines on white paper.

He would constantly and untiringly exhort his disciples to cherish the property of the Triple Jewel. Like a compassionate parent, he feared that out of ignorance we would create karma, which we would later find too difficult to bear. He was so careful not to waste even a drop of water on himself, demonstrating for us how to be frugal. But in giving to living beings to quicken their Bodhi minds, he was the richest of kings and would travel the world untiringly to gather in the smallest potential.

I especially remember him as a flawlessly pure, awesome Bhikshu displaying the inconceivable, unutterable, multidimensional Flower Adornment World. Each word, line, and phrase of the Sutra described the Master himself! Yet he was always careful to never put on a special, grandiose style. He simply was magnificent, without trying to be. He was also always careful to warn us that spiritual penetrations are not so important. Over, and over, and over again, he used his breath and energy to praise the pure precepts and straight cultivation. He taught us to maintain an ordinary, human mind, whatever states we encountered, and not to be distracted by thinking we had something. He kept us sane; he kept us true; he kept us on the straight and broad road to Bodhi.

An unlettered and dim-witted person like me could never finish describing his virtues. My heart aches that I cannot express his compassion and wisdom, and his awesome, magnificent personality. We should all make the vow to always find him, to see him, to hear him speak Dharma, until we arrive at Bodhi. Only then will he truly be happy. Only then can we repay his kindness.

To say this in verse:

He gave up the rewards of his homeland, but not his loyalty to it.
Not taking a drop for himself he amassed boundless blessings
Which he gave with delight to beings
So they might ascend to Bodhi.

He constantly tended his garden
Of tender Bodhi Sprouts:
He would weed them, prune them, and encourage them
To grow big, healthy, and strong.

Whenever a Bodhi sprout would say,
"I don't want to grow anymore, I've had it!"
He'd smile kindly, and let it be.
He labored not for a reward.

He cherished and saved the most simple things:
Tissue paper, water, electricity.
He dared not waste the tiniest object,
But in giving he was the richest of kings.

With infinite, genuine patience
He'd wait for just the right time,
And then speak a few words of wisdom,
Precisely right on the mark.

In this way, he gradually raised us.
Each one at his own rate of learning
He tested us, and if we did fail,
He repeated the lesson again, no problem!

We'd run to him with our bruises.
Then he would calm us down,
And explain to us how to do things,
Without always stumbling and falling.

Appearances could not fool him;
He insisted on the truth.
Yet sometimes he'd let things go by,
For those who weren't ready to take it.

Compassionate parent, he exhorted us,
"Don't do any evil, offer up all good!"
Hoping to wake us up from our folly,
So that we might escape the inferno.

He feared neither hunger, cold, nor death;
There was only one thing he feared:
He feared for the pitiful masses of beings
Who toss in the sea of suffering.

It's so hard to truly describe him,
For he left not a trace of himself.
Nor was there a trace of self
In anything that he did.

His state too high to be seen,
Yet his actions so natural and plain.
He did not want to mesmerize people;
He just wanted to help them be sane.

With precepts as his substance,
And the appearance of a pure Bhikshu,
Extracting the principles from the specifics,
He applied them to new situations.

In the arts, sciences, and literature,
In every kind of learning and skill,
The Master of all Masters was he,
Yet never was he pretentious.

Every small and great matter we'd bring him,
To be solved by his great wisdom.
With great kindness he would consider,
Then surprise us with just the right answer!

94

He could see hidden talent quite clearly,
Then nurture it to become full.
He cared about others' advancement,
Not for his own reputation.

His manner of teaching was markless:
No Teacher, no student, no lesson.
And yet when graduation time came,
The learning had all taken place.

Although his patience was endless,
He demanded the best quality,
And with each step we'd take on the Path,
He'd be with us to further us on.

A vast treasury lay in his bosom:
Precious gems, a spectacular array.
If you are sincere, and try your best,
He will show one especially for you!

But these gems he does not show casually;
He would not throw pearls before swine.
He saves and protects them, knowing their worth,
Till we can appreciate them.

Some say he's beyond all emotion:
Beyond happiness and beyond grief.
That every facial expression
Is a response to the needs of beings.

That may be quite true, indeed,
I haven't the wisdom to say.
Yet from my human perspective,
I have seen him truly delighted.

Whenever one of his students
Would bring forth the true Bodhi mind,
I believe he would truly be happy,
I believe then he felt satisfied.

Whenever one of his students,
Would genuinely cultivate,
His expression would always be special,
Not like at other times.

As for tears, sometimes he cried.
Once he wept and explained:
"As I bestow this Dharma upon you,
I already know you won't practice."

Another time he cried
in front of professors and teachers,
When he learned that the youth of today,
No longer have the will to live.

When we feel no one understands us,
We feel lonely, and in deep despair,
He speaks a few words of kindness
To teach us not to be selfish.

To him we bring all our sorrows,
And he takes them on to himself.
But not a single worry or trouble,
Would he pass on to anyone else.

Even when in great pain and so spent,
He would raise his great heroic vigor.
To light up a magnanimous smile,
Not wanting to cause us to worry.

Knowing dharmas and beings are empty,
He could simply have left all the trouble,
But he went through such pain and trouble,
Riding on the power of vows.

Not until all beings attain Bodhi,
Will he ever, ever rest.
Not coming, not going, thus, thus, unmoving,
How can he truly be known?

Some say Amitabha, some say Gwan Yin,
Or Earth Store Bodhisattva is he;
Or Confucius the father of teachers,
Or other Sage-heroes of men.

How could one man be many?
That truly is hard to conceive of!
Is it because he embodies the virtue
Possessed by all such Great Ones?

I so dull and dim-witted
Could not finish praising his virtues.
This black ink upon white paper
Falls so short, and fails to describe him.

But anyone wanting to know
What the Great Master Hsuan Hua was like,
Can start with the great Flower Adornment
That King most high among Sutras.

For there's not a word in that Sutra
That the Master did not reveal
And personify in every aspect
This I firmly and truly believe.

And one more thing should be known,
Every Word that came from his mouth
Was the Truth, like it or not!
Moreover, he really did it himself!

THE
MASTER'S
GIFT
TO US

ᘓ   Frederick Klarer
(Guo Hu)

Three incidents of my years with the Abbot stand out in my mind and have served as a basis for my practice. Because they may be of interest to others, I relate them below. The first was in fall/winter of 1970-71.

Following the summer session of 1970, there were perhaps as many as fifteen men living and practicing at the Buddhist Lecture Hall on Waverly Place in San Francisco's China-town. A similar number of women lived in a private home not too far away and spent their days at the Buddhist Lecture Hall. At any given moment there could be twenty or more people crowded into that one room. To escape the crowding, several of the men had moved up onto the roof, where we built sleeping boxes out of wooden packing crates and slept built sleeping boxes out of wooden packing crates and slept sitting up. This was the beginning period of cultivation for all of us, a first attempt, and tensions ordinarily ran high, as we each struggled with our private demons and projected them out on each other. As the cold of winter closed in, the tension became unbearable. We each began to fantasize of a wonderful, quite, spacious forest monastery, where we could do nothing but cultivate day and night and would be free of the supposed obstacles of the Buddhist Lecture Hall. That fantasy quickly blossomed into an obsession for some of us.

Then, one evening, after the formal sutra lecture, the Abbot announced that he had a special present for us. He laughed in his inimitable way, his eyes twinkled, and we all slavered in anticipation. He told us that we would have to wait, that it would be a Christmas present, but that it would be something beyond price—the best present that we would ever receive.

During this period we had been looking at real estate all over California, and beyond. Some of us clever ones quickly put the disparate facts together and decided that the Abbot was going to give us a wonderful mountain monastery for Christmas. Once we had figured that out, anticipation grew daily. As we looked at various country properties we delighted in the anticipation. Life would be wonderful. We would have the perfect circumstances to cultivate. All the obstacles facing us would disappear with a move to a perfect environment and all would be well.

As Christmas approached the Abbot would remind us of the gift that we could expect and we all became happier and happier, expecting our new toys for Christmas. At last the Abbot announced that, on a certain day, he would give us our present. The night of that lecture the Buddhist Lecture Hall was packed. Everyone was there, each anticipating the evitable announcement that we were all moving to the country for the perfect contemplative life. The Abbot delivered the evening lecture, as usual. The translators finished translating. The Abbot lectured again and, once again, the translators finished translating. Still no mention of our country monastery. We were all beginning to worry a bit. The Venerable Shr Fu put his hands together to recite the transference of merit—then stopped. "Oh." he said. He had forgotten. Today was the day he would give us our present. We all sighed a great sigh of relief. The end to our problems was at hand.

The Venerable Shr Fu then said, "Today I am giving each of you two beautiful, hand-written scrolls. They are a precious gift that you must never put down." This wasn't a monastery, but it was a good start. At least something special and valuable. He continued, "On the first scroll is written "Birth." On the second scroll is written "Death." You are to hang those scrolls, one behind each eyelid, so that you see them at every moment. If you are able to see those scrolls at every moment, you will certainly attain enlightenment in this very lift."

We were all taken aback. That was all well and good, but was this a joke? Surely there was more. Then Shr Fu laughed, and looked out over the assembly, and then made as if to speak again. Clearly, that was not the main event. The big present was yet to come. He continued, "But if you are going to meditate night and day you will need a place to do it. You will need a Ch'an Hall." Ah, we each thought, now comes the real present— what we have all been waiting for all these months—the country awaits. "To mediate you will need a Ch'an Hall," At last, this is it we all thought. He continued, "For the pillars of your Ch'an Hall, I give you the four directions; for its roof, the sky. For your sitting mat I give you the broad earth." He beamed at us, as if he had just opened a box of the lost luscious chocolates and offered each of us the best one in the box. He then continued. "You have your topic, you have your place. Now—WORK!!" He then laughed his inimitable laugh, put his palms together, and began to recite the transference of merit. We were all in a state of shock—stunned. Ch'an humor was onething—but this was serious. The evening's lecture ended and we were each left with our private thoughts. Some thought the whole event a big Ch'an joke—designed to shake us out of attachments. Others were simply disappointed. Each one of us dealt with our disappointment, our shock, in a different way, and the event passed into the past. A few months later we purchased the property at 11731 Fifteenth Street and began to build a new place for cultivation in earnest. Gold Mountain Monastery came into being.

I have thought over that story many, many times, and slowly understood the precious gift that Shr Fu offered each of us that day. It has taken me more then twenty years to begin to make use of that gift, but it still is as fresh as one of those imagined chocolates when the box was first opened. Every moment, every place, every event, is nothing but opportunity to cultivate, if we have the heart and resolve to experience life that way. Entrance into the Dharma-realm is available at every moment; we need simply to recognize our constant opportunities. I have related this story because a gift takes its real meaning when it is passed onto another. For those who were absent that day, I pass on Shr Fu's gift, and hope that you will make better used of it then I have.

The second incident that I constantly recall was a trip that Heng Ch'ien, Heng Shou, and I took to look at property in Northern California, Oregon, and Idaho. We were traveling in a Volkswagen bus, sleeping in the bus or camping, looking at various possible sites for a country monastery. Finally, after we had located a few sites that Shr Fu, with whom Heng Ch'ien had communicated by telephone, thought sounded promising, he came up to meet us and spent a couple of days with us driving around. One morning we had stopped by a beautiful stream in northern Idaho to make our one meal of the day, Shr Fu, as was his practice when traveling, ate virtually nothing—a banana and perhaps another piece of fruit. I was, at the time, practicing eating at a single sitting, and made sure that I ate enough to last the better part of the kalpa before I had to get up or the clock hit noon. Heng Ch'ien and Heng Shou, neither of whom had any great interest in food, wandered away from where we had stopped and set up our meal, over to side of the stream, and were idly skipping rocks over the surface of the water, taking a well deserved rest from hours of driving. Shr Fu and I sat together on a log, he eating his banana and I eating everything that I could get my hands on. Shr Fu was watching Heng Ch'ien and Heng Shou skip rocks, and asked me what it was about skipping rocks on water. He asked if there were any good at it and I gave my evaluation. He then said to me, "Why don't you go play with your friends? Sounding like a solicitous parent, concerned that I had been left out. I replied that, when it was time to eat, I ate; that "I knew what was important." He turned his head to me with a delighted twinkle in his eye, "Oh, you know what is important. Kuo Hu knows what is important. Kuo Hu knows what is important." He repeated the phrase over and over again, chuckling. He then finished his banana and went over to Heng Ch'ien and Heng Shou, announcing to them as he came, "I have something important to tell you. This is very important. Kuo Hu knows what is important. Kuo Hu knows what is important." I sat and ate, very pleased with myself for knowing what was important, eating when it was time to eat rather than wasting my time at play. While I ate Shr Fu stood to one side of Heng Ch'ien and Heng Shou, watching them continue to skip rocks. After watching a few throws Shr Fu stepped a couple of feet away, examined the ground carefully, and picked up a large, irregularly shaped stone weighing at least several pounds. He then walked up to the stream's edge and heaved the stone in. It sank without a trace. He then looked directly at Heng Ch'ien and Heng Shou, who were watching the ripples spread to Shr Fu. The three of them stood there for a moment, looking at each other, then all laughed at the same time. The three of them then ambled back to where I was still eating. Shr Fu telling them both very earnesly how I knew what was important. Heng Ch'ien and Heng Shou then had their lunch as well. I finished eating, then went over to the stream's edge and skipped several stones with great skill, demonstrating, once I had finished the important matter, my prowess with secondary matters as well.

From then on, at each property we examined, Shr Fu would very seriously turn to me and ask my opinion of the property, announcing, "Kuo Hu knows what is important." When we all eventually returned to Gold

Mountain. Shr Fu announced on several occasions when we were discussing some problem, that everyone should ask me, since "Kuo Hu knows what is important." Eventually that particular teaching died down and life went on. But I have considered that incident many, many times. Shr Fu's real teaching there was a demonstration of sympathy with living beings. He recognized what was important to each of us, whether it was self-importance and eating, or relating from hard work by skipping rocks across a stream, and responded to each with as much teaching as was possible. What was really important was not, as I felt at the time, my self-discipline, but rather to recognize that Shr Fu taught each of us individually, and that what was most important was to recognize what teaching was for me and what was for someone else—to not confuse the two, to not expect someone else to live up to what he had taught me to strive for, and to not seek to strive for someone else's goals. That teaching was a deep and vivid expression of compassion and bodhicitta (*Bodhi mind*), and one that, as I have slowly come to understand, that I seek to emulate in every moment.

The third incident that has stuck with me all these years occurred while we were building Gold Mountain, at Fifteenth Street. The building was an old mattress factory, full of years of dirt and dust. We were able to clean it up to a great extent, but a problem that seemed insurmountable was that of the brick walls themselves. The building had been cheaply built, and the bricks were a bit crumbly. Much worse, the mortar was crumbling. The building wasn't about to fall down, but every brush against the walls brought bits of mortar and sand. There was no way to keep the interior clean if we could not solve this problem. Heng Ch'ien brought the problem to Shr Fu's attention, and he instantly had a solution. He ordered a bucket brought, some pure cement, water, and old broom. He had us mix a very thin solution of fement in water. He then took the broom, dipped it into the bucket, and then slammed the soaked broom againts the brick wall. A few experiments with more or less cement, different stroke techniques, and a couple of old brooms, and he pronounced the process a success. He carefully instructed us to mix the cement with the water in precisely the proportions he had established, use an old broom against the walls as he had demonstrated. We then split up into several work groups and proceeded with the task. However, it quickly became apparent that the solution was so thin that most of it dripped down and off the walls. It looked as if it would take forever to cover all the walls. So one of us got the bright idea to thicken the mixture a bit so that it would hold better. Sure enough, the thickened mixture went on much more easily and covered much more quickly. The process would not take nearly as long as we had feared. We also discovered that a new broom, which would hold a greater load of mixture, sped up the process even more. Once again, modern American, ingenuity and know-how would save the day.

Some time later Shr Fu came by to see how we were doing. One look and he exploded, "Stupid, really stupid," he exclaimed. That's not how to do it." We objected, explaining all the advantages of our improvements. He just repeated, "Stupid, really stupid." Sure enough, as the mixture dried on the walls, where we had used the thin mixture and the old broom the pure cement dried into a hard, very thin coating that subsequently lasted for years. Where we had used the thicker mixture and the new broom the coating dried as thick flakes that could be easily picked or peeled off. Eventually we had to remove all of those sections and do them over. Our attempt at efficiency caused nothing but more work and a waste of resources. What was so important about that teaching was not Shr Fu's knowledge of wall coating techniques—I am not sure whether he had ever used that technique before or not. What was important was the clarity—the concentration and insight—that he applied to the task. He perceived directly what the problem was, exactly how much was enough to solve that problem, and applied just the right amount to solve it. He pointed out to us exactly how to apply the techniques of cultivation. It is that ability to perceive a situation as it truly is, not otherwise, that directs one's cultivation to be most effective. Recognizing precisely what needs to be done, the appropriate tools for the task, and the proper application lies at the heart of what Shr Fu taught. Again, it has taken me most of my life simply to recognize this lesson and to begin to apply it in my own work.

I have sought to cultivate according to those simple lessons that Shr Fu taught. To understand that there is only one issue—that of birth and death—and that every moment of every day in every place is the right time and the right place to resolve that issue, that doing one's own work, and not someone else's is the job at hand, and one cannot understand the mind or actions of a sage with respect to others if one does not even understand them with respect to oneself, and finally, that the tools of cultivation are useful only when one understands the problem to be solved, selects the appropriate tools, and applies them properly, and that concentration and insight are the means to that realization. With these words I am simply passing along three of my experiences with Shr Fu, hoping that the record of those experiences will benefit others, as they have been of such benefit to me. If there were others present at those occurrences who remember them differently, I can only apologize for my partial perception and experience and trust that they will correct my report. I have repeated those experiences as faithfully as I remember them.

BRINGING FORTH
THE RESOLVE
FOR THE
UNSURPASSED WAY

ು Shr Heng Cheng

I met the Venerable Master in October 1976 at Gold Mountain Monastery in San Francisco when I was attending college. I had been involved with psychology and philosophy on the campus I was attending, and one day my philosophy instructor gave me a list of spiritual centers in San Francisco. The second place I went to was Gold Mountain.

At that time I went, the Master was lecturing on *The Flower Adornment Sutra*. I did not understand anything that was going on. However, I knew at that time that the Master was my teacher. The second or third time that I went to Gold Mountain Monastery, I saw the Venerable Master sitting on the Dharma Seat as a five-year-old child. I was invited to go with the Bhikshunis to take a look at the new Way-place in Talmage, California. There was a group of Korean students who came to visit Gold Mountain Monastery, and so the Venerable Master took them to the City of Ten Thousand Buddhas. I liked the place immediately, and the Master also knew this. It was very cold that day, and I took my heavy coat with me, but I didn't need it. Everyone was hovering around the heater in one of the rooms up at Dragon Tree House, but I was very warm without the heater. Later, I was to return to San Francisco in the same car with the Master, but I stood outside waiting to find out in what car I was supposed to return.

The Master was already in the car, and asked, "Kuo K'ai, are you going to stay here?"

During the Winter Semester Break, I attended my first Buddha Recitation Session at Gold Mountain. As I remember, this was my second personal encounter with the Venerable Master. I took refuge with the Triple Jewel during this time, and within two or three days I wanted to leave the home-life. I spoke with one of the nuns at that time, and I was granted an audience with the Master. A Bhikshuni acted as the translator for me. One of the first things the Venerable Master asked me was, "Do you have a boyfriend?" I expressed my wish to leave the home-life, and the Master replied that he wanted me to finish school, and that he wanted to watch me for a while. I had only six months left of school, and was planning to continue my studies in psychology by transferring to a major university. After that Buddha Recitation Session, and upon returning to my apartment, I began to mentally and physically make arrangements to leave home after I graduated in June.

Early in the spring of 1977 there was a Dharma gathering at San Francisco's Golden Gate Park to pray for the ending of a serious drought in California. At the end of the day, some of us returned to Gold Mountain Monastery. I came face to face with the Master, and directly said, "You came back."

On June 25, 1977, I went to the women's Way-place with my belongings, and a week later moved to the City of Ten Thousand Buddhas to help start the first summer school at the City. It was during this summer--one and a half months later— that I left the home-life. I took a bus back to San Francisco, and the event took place at Gold Mountain Monastery on the anniversary of Guan Shr Yin Bodhisattva's Enlightenment. Someone told me that I looked like a soldier during that day. After the ceremony, the Venerable Master told me that I couldn't get angry any more. Two days later, I returned to the City, and the person I was working with asked me, "Well, how does it feel to leave home?" I immediately replied, "You know, I don't feel that I have done anything different." The next time that the Master came to the City, she told him what I said, and he laughted and said that I had been a cultivator in the past. Between the winter of 1979 on through to the end of June 1990, I was in a situation which forced me to take a good look at myself, and to learn what I was really supposed to be doing as a left-home person. What was really memorable for me during this time was that I was able to observe the Venerable Master's all-encompassing virtuous conduct. As I now try to write this, I must admit that there is no real way to express what has happened to me because of such a teacher.

I have been memorizing *The Wonderful Dharma Lotus Flower Sutra* now for many years, and have observed the Venerable One's adornments through my memorization. Not only have I been able to "taste" the wonderful flavor of this Sutra, but my reverence and respect for the Venerable Master has greatly transformed me.

I also learned how important it is to attend the Dharma activities that the Venerable Master has established in the Hall of Ten Thousand Buddhas. I have mentioned to others that, "In times of difficulty, the safest place to be is in the Buddha Hall." Often times, I try to repay the Venerable Master's great kindness and compassion by transferring the merit from work that was difficult for me to do, to the Master. The last time that I did this in the presence of the Master was during the Jeweled Repentance before the Ten Thousand Buddhas in 1990. The Master had come into the Buddha Hall at the end of a day's session. He stood about four rows of bowing cushions in front of me and looked directly at me with a smile on his face. After the above session took place, I experienced something of such awesome magnitude with regard to the Venerable Master's great spiritual powers that I cannot present it here. However, during these past eleven and a half years, my faith, reverence, and respect for the Triple Jewel have increased to such a degree that I don't want anything to prevent me from going forward in my cultivation for the Unsurpassed Way of all Buddhas.

There are verses at the end of Chapter Four of *The Wonderful Dharma Lotus Flower Sutra* in which the Venerable Mahakashyapa talkes about the difficulty in repaying the Buddha's kindness. I believe that this is also true with a Good Knowing Advisor. Just in these past almost eighteen years, I ask myself how am I going to repay my teacher's kindness and patience with me for so many years? The debt of kindness only increases day by day. It is easy to say, "If I had known then, what I know now...." I remember that when the Master first started teaching Americans, someone told him that this is an impossible task. However, I am an American, born and raised in the San Francisco Bay Area. Although I have made many serious and not so serious mistakes in the past, and will make many more in the future, I can firmly and confidently say that the Venerable Master has taught and transformed me in many ways. He has been my teacher in the past, in the present, and will be my teacher throughout all of future time until I myself embody *The Wonderful Dharma Lotus Flower Sutra* and the power of Guan Shr Yin Bodhisattva. Only then will I truly be able to help him in his work.

INVESTIGATING
CHAN AND
SEEING
THE BUDDHA

ca Sun Dongbo

Seventeen years ago (1978), my year of study in America ended.

On December 22, I went to Gold Mountain Monastery, which was still on Fifteenth Street then. Compared to temples in Taiwan, Gold Mountain Monastery appeared very poor and humble.

I couldn't find the front door of the monastery. Standing in front of what looked like both a door and a window, I couldn't decided what to do. Suddenly, waves of warm energy passed through my chest and spread through my body. All of a sudden, I became very alert and clear-minded. Someone inside waved to me and stepped out through a small door on the right side. A Caucasian monk spoke a few simple sentences in Chinese to me, telling me he was an American disciple of the Venerable Master. I indicated that I wished to attend the three-week Winter Chan Session at the Sagely City of Ten Thousand Buddhas. The Dharma Master led me inside with a smile. I saw a few Chinese people and a young Englishman who had just arrived from London for the Chan Session. The five people, including me, got a ride to the City of Ten Thousand Buddhas. On the way there they said, "In the Chan Sessions at the City of Ten Thousand Buddhas, laypeople have never managed to stay for more than two or three days."

I had recited the Buddha's name for fifteen years, but I had never participated in a Chan Session before. All of a sudden, I felt very uneasy. Just what was a Chan Session all about? What were they hinting at?

In the winter, it became dark quite early. At dusk, in the car I smelled a very heavy and strong scent of sandalwood, which didn't disperse for a long time. We drove for another half an hour before reaching our destination.

The City of Ten Thousand Buddhas was very poor and humble then. During the Chan Session, every night the Venerable Master would lecture on a short passage from the *Flower Adornment Sutra* and give an instructional talk. In the evening of the second Sunday, the Venerable Master said he needed to make a trip to Los Angeles the next day. That night, he especially spoke a four-line verse:

> *In 1978, we hold a Chan Session.*
> *Be neither fast nor slow, and don't get nervous.*
> *Continuously and without a break, be diligent and vigorous.*
> *Soon you will reach the Buddhas' ground.*

He also instructed us: "In investigating Chan, one should not be afraid and one should not be lax. Among you, someone will definitely realize one of the Dharma-doors of the Twenty-five Kinds of Perfect Penetrations.

When I was bowing to the Buddhas after the lecture, I saw five large Buddhas sitting in the air at the level of the Venerable Master's shoulders. A purple-golden aura brought his red sash into relief as the colors inter-reflected.

After bowing to the Buddhas, the Venerable Master asked, "Did any of you see any responses? Speak up and tell everyone about it." I felt the Master's question was rather peculiar. I also vaguely remember the Master saying, "If you have any responses in cultivation, don't speak about them, unless your Master agrees or encourages fellow cultivators to do so, but even then, you should just touch upon them," and so forth.

The Venerable Master seemed to know that I was confused. he asked two more times. I still vacillated. Finally, he said, "Speak up and let everyone know that the merit and virtue of Chan meditation is absolutely not in vain." I finally spoke.

When I was bowing to the Buddhas, I looked up. Above the stage where the Venerable Master was sitting, at the height of the Master's shoulders, there were five cylindrically shaped Buddhas with purple-golden bodies about ten feet tall, sitting in full lotus in mid-air. At the time, I was about a hundred feet from the stage.

To tell the truth, the Venerable Master did not make a deep impression on me during those two weeks of Chan. It was only when I saw the Buddhas that I suddenly woke up. In such a humble Way-place, what kind of virtue did the Venerable Master have to receive the protection of five Buddhas?

****

Venerable Master, you have suddenly gone. The disciples at the Sagely City have suddenly lost the one they relied on. Everyone is distressed and flustered. In this Dharma-ending Age, deviant teachers and deviant theories are everywhere. The spreading of evil dharmas is frightening to see, deluding disciples of the Buddha, hindering them from bringing forth the resolve for Bodhi, and seriously harming students of Buddhism.

Venerable Master, you alone know that I kept hesitating and didn't want to write or speak about my experience. In 1984, you encouraged me to translate Sutras and said that after a book was printed, you would reward me with an honorary degree. But after I translated twenty pages of the *Sixth Patriarch's Dharma Jewel Platform Sutra*, in 1986 I had a vision in which the Sixth Patriarch Hui Neng warned me, "Don't contend, and you will naturally find peace." Therefore for nine years, I have followed the principle of taking care of myself and hiding my light—I neither spoke nor wrote.

But this time, I didn't need you to ask me. This ought to be the time when I cannot refuse to repay the kindness of the Buddhas and the Venerable Master. This article "Investigating Chan and Seeing the Buddha" will be published in the two books *The Venerable Master Hsuan Hua To Lun— Responses and Deeds and Chan Is the Only Truth* (in 1983, Patriarch Bodhidharma instructed me to do this).

Venerable Master, I will tell the public about my experiences in studying Buddhism and what I have gained from cultivation. The first reason is to repay the Buddhas' kindness and to thank you for setting a good example, battling resolutely in the face of hardship, sacrificing yourself for the Dharma, establishing a City of Dharma, and protecting the Proper Dharma in this evil environment. Your every word and deed, your spirit and example, serve as a standard for those of future generations to follow. Secondly, I wish to encourage people by telling them how wonderful and sublime the City of Ten Thousand Buddhas is. Buddhists who investigate Chan and cultivate at the City of Ten Thousand Buddhas constantly receive the great spiritual aid and mindful protection of all Buddhas. It is truly a Way-place of the Proper Dharma which is rarely found in the world. Genuine Buddhists ought to sacrifice themselves to protect this City of Dharma. Thirdly, I wish to encourage the disciples at the Sagely City not to be moved by changes in people and affairs, to rely on the Venerable Master's teachings, fulfill their responsibilities, honestly practice, guard and protect the City of Dharma, and be at ease within the Dharma.

Venerable Master, although you are not the Master I study under (I disagree with some of your teachings, and I hardly ever drew near to you; none of your disciples know me), your lofty integrity and your stubborn determination win my praise and endless admiration. I didn't learn any Buddhadharma from you, Venerable Master. All I learned was your "hard bones" spirit. If one's bones are not hard, it's difficult to attain the Buddha Way. Even if someone were to kill you, slice you up and eat you, Venerable Master, you'd probably say, "I'm not dead!" Disciples at the Sagely City, after the Venerable Master's completion of stillness, he is still the same as he has always been. At a time when I needed it most, he inspired and taught me. He's truly a compassionate Bodhisattva!

Venerable Master, how could death touch you?

I hope this brief article will give some revelations and thoughts to the assembly.

Finally, I wish the fourfold assembly at the Sagely City boundless Dharma joy!

Namo Amitabha Buddha!

THE VENERABLE MASTER'S GIFTS FROM THE HEART

෪   Shr Heng Sure

All of you who have come to attend the Memorial Ceremony in Praise and Recognition of the Venerable Master Hua's Kindness have probably been drawn here by the Master's eighteen great vows, just as iron filings are drawn to a magnet.

Some people say that Master was a Bodhisattva who came to the world on his vows, but the Master firmly denied this. He said,

> I'm just like a tiny ant, mosquito, or a horse. I'm like a
> road that all Buddhists, the followers of all religions,
> and all living beings can walk on to reach supreme Bodhi
> and the Land of Ultimate Bliss.

This statement reveals the Master's spirit. Everyone think for a moment: If the Master really is a Bodhisattva, how can we tell?

Bodhisattvas practice the six perfections and the myriad conducts. The first perfection, as you all know, is giving. There are three kinds: the giving of wealth, of fearlessness, and, the highest kind, of Dharma. Let's take a look at the Master's conduct. From the very first day I met him until he finally left the world, the Master gave constantly. He paid tuition for students who couldn't afford it, donated Sutras to libraries lacking them, and started schools for people who had no opportunity to study. He practiced giving to perfection.

He gave blessings to every disciple and every faithful followers. In what way? The Master founded the City of Ten Thousand Buddha, the International Translation Institute, and twenty-seven branch temples. He gave us the precious storehouse of Buddhadharma, the pure precepts that protect our Dharma body and wisdom life, and our great resolves for Bodhi.

He also gave us Dharma-selecting vision, the ability to distinguish between proper and deviant, so that we would be able to follow the ultimate truth of the Middle Way and not go astray, or encounter demonic or karmic obstacles. The Venerable Master transmitted the path of the ancients, the "ultimate truth of the Middle Way," to us, and yet he never expected anyone to thank him.

For those of us who left the home-life and practiced under his guidance, the Master purified our minds of defilement. The Master gave to the world the six guiding principles—no fighting, no greed, no seeking, no selfishness, no pursuit of personal gain, and no lying. These principles are the Mind Ground Dharma-door; they can make our minds pure and bright. Such is the perfection of giving practiced by Bodhisattvas. The Master gave to each of us the Dharma-door we like to practice, enabling us to plant blessings, merit, and virtue. All we have to do is accept this gift with open arms.

Once, taking advantage of a spare moment, I requested instruction from the Master. The Master said in surprise,

> You're seeking instruction too? Don't seek outside, not even the slightest bit. When you can finally stop seeking, you'll be liberated. 'When you reach the place of no seeking, there are no worries.' That's enough!

Then he smiled and added,

> I have come to this country, or you could say to this
> world, hoping that someone will bring forth a great
> Bodhi resolve. When that happens, I will have achieved
> my aim.

On the day that each of you brings forth a great Bodhi resolve, you will have fulfilled the Master's aim in giving from his heart.

Using Virtue to Convert People and Propagate the Dharma in the West

Most people are drawn by the stories of the Venerable Master's miraculous responses and extraordinary powers. But the Master told us,

> In the West, we should not speak of spiritual powers,
> because most people are educated in the scientific
> tradition and if you tell them about things that they
> cannot see or hear, they won't believe you. What should
> the emphasis be on? Virtue. We have to teach virtue in
> the West, and there were be a responses in their hearts.

And so in America, the subject of superhuman spiritual powers is seldom discussed. Tonight I'd like to share an experience which shows how virtue can influence people.

I was on the road for nearly three years, making a pilgrimage to the City of Ten Thousand Buddhas. When I reached the City, I continued to hold a vow of silence. Since I did not speak, or read or write letters, I completely cut of all contact with my parents and relatives. I feared that my mother was at home worrying that her son had been brainwashed by some cult, for there were rumors going around that the Master had kidnapped his American disciples and was giving them drugs. Little did she know that I had shaved my head and stopped speaking because I had been touched by the Venerable Master's cultivation and wanted to diligently work on my practice. My mother probably thought she'd lost her son; she had no idea of what leaving the home-life to join the Sangha was all about. So, when I reached the City of Ten Thousand Buddhas, my mother was determined to visit me and see what kind of freak her son had become.

I remember very clearly that my mother came quite late in the evening, when it was already dark. When I went to the office (of the City of Ten Thousand Buddhas), someone said, "Hey, guess what? Your mother's here!" Still holding a vow of silence, I went in to take a look. My mother had been crying, judging from her tear-streaked face. The Master was speaking to her and holding her hand, consoling her and telling her in English, "Don't cry." Although he didn't know English, he was speaking to her in English, without relying on a translator. When he saw me, he said, "There's no need for you to be here. I can take care of this." Strange! Although my mother looked slightly scared, there was something else on her face—an expression of reverence. I left the office. Since I was involved in a Dharma session a few days later, I didn't get to see my mother again, and she went home.

After a couple of years, when my vow of silence was over, I began to speak again. At that time, the Master invited my mother to come celebrate her fiftieth birthday at the City of Ten Thousand Buddhas. He said it was the first time a Bhikshu's mother had been invited to celebrate her birthday in a monastery. The Master asked all the girls in Instilling Goodness Elementary School to make cards for Guan Yin Bodhisattva's Birthday for my mother. That day, my mother received over thirty birthday cards with pictures, couplets, and short verses of Guan Yin Bodhisattva drawn and written by the little girls. She was very touched and said, "Why, I know who Guan Yin Bodhisattva is!" When the Master invited her to speak to the assembly, she said, "All of you monks and nuns should know that your elderly Master is a very wise person. He gave me a string of recitation beads and told me to recite, 'Namo Guan Shr Yin Bodhisattva,' and that's what I've done."

Afterwards, my mother related what had happened the first day. "You know, I was very scared the frist time I came to the City. I thought they might have drugged my tea, and that if I drank it I might also become bald like you. When I got here, I just started crying. Then your Master came out and shook hands with me. Although I was very nervous, deep down in my heart I seemed to understand what the Master was saying to me. Then the Master invited me to sit in his golfcart (which he drove around the City of Ten Thousand Buddhas because the place was so big). That evening, he looked straight at me and said,

> You should be happy you have a Bhikshu for a son.
> Your son has followed me for life after life. You haven't
> lost a son; you've gained a monk. You should be grateful.
> Your son will have many things to do.

What do yo think he meant by this?" I didn't understand either. But if the master wasn't using virtue to influence my mother, then what was he using? Not spiritual powers, that's for sure. He was using plain sincerity. My mother, a Christain, had already stepped onto the Buddha path that day. She even recited "Namo Guan Shi Yin Bodhisattva" and had recitation beads. There's a couplet about the Venerable Master which describes his spirit in propagating the Dharma to benefit living beings, be it in Hong Kong, Taiwan, or America. It goes:

> *His kindness and compassion cross over all;*
> *Believers are liberated and perfect the Right Enlightenment.*
> *Transforming beings wherever he goes, his spirit remains intact;*
> *Those who venerate him obtain blessings and awaken to the*
> *Unproduced.*

119

"CUT OFF DESIRE!"

cs   Shr Heng You

Today, I feel kind of happy, and I also feel kind of sad. I'm happy to be together with all of you great, wise teachers. But on the other hand, I feel kind of sad. In the past, when I came to the City of Ten Thousand Buddhas and Gold Mountain Monastery, I was often asked to come up and speak about my understanding of Buddhism. During those times, a certain person always sat there. Sometimes he would just listen to me quietly without saying anything. At other times, he would correct me or make some comments. Today, I'm sitting here, but that person is no longer here. He will never again correct me or teach me. It's really rare to find someone who can correct your mistakes for you. Now I've lost that person, who was my teacher and also your teacher.

I am not as fortunate as those of you who live at the City of Ten Thousand Buddhas and Gold Mountain Monastery, who were often with the Master and heard his teachings. Because of my heavy karmic obstacles, I had to struggle to make a living out in the world. I couldn't come to the City of Ten Thousand Buddhas to be near the Master. Because of that, I really treasured the few sentences that the Master did speak to me. Because they were so rare, I tried my best to apply them in my life. Because the Master's words to me were so few, they were extremely precious to me.

120

In April 1977, I went to Canada to present a paper on Mechanics at a seven-day conference. Afterwards, I went to Gold Mountain Monastery to see the Master. As soon as I saw him, I felt a great sense of familiarity. Gold Mountain Monastery was on Fifteenth Street then, and somehow I felt that I'd been there before. I had never seen a monk or entered a Buddhist temple before. That was the first time I came into contact with Buddhism and met a monk—the Venerable Master. I had to go out to make a living when I was only twelve years old. It was extremely tough. From the time I was twelve, I never bowed to anyone or even had the thought of bowing to anyone. But as soon as I saw the Master, I had an indescribable feeling of ease and familiarity, as if I'd returned home. Probably you all have caring families, so you cannot imagine how I felt. No one can know that feeling but myself. I immediately bowed to the Master. The Master laughed and said, "Look, here's a professor bowing to me!"

After bowing down and getting up, I felt like a different person. I used to be a very stubborn and unsubmissive person. How could I have bowed to a monk? I can't describe my feeling. A sudden change had occurred in me. I was very happy, and I took the refuge with the Master that same day. At about ten o'clock that night, after everyone had gone to sleep, I sat on the bench in the Buddhahall. My mind was blank. I was in a daze—I can't describe my feeling. Then the Master walked over and sat down beside me. I didn't say a word, nor did he. We sat there for about ten minutes, and all of a sudden he shouted, "Cut off desire!" I was not scared, and I didn't move, but his hollering of "cut off desire" was like a lion's roar. It made a deep impression on me. I will never forget it! I learned Buddhism from the *Sixth Patriarch Platform Sutra,* which doesn't mention desire directly, but says, "The mind of lust is basically the cause for the mind of purity." That time, the idea of "cutting off desire" really impressed me. Desire was truly my great illness, but I didn't realize it before. From that day on, I recognized this illness. I worked on that teaching for many years. I applied effect constantly, and it was very difficult. It affected not only me, but my whole family. Later on, I realized that the cutting off of desire is the Buddha's basic teaching in all the Sutras. That was the first teaching the Master gave me.

The following year, 1978, I joined the Master's delegation on a six-week visit to Southeast Asia. That was the longest time I was near the Master and also the time when I received the most teachings. Here, I'll just mention one thing that happened.

We went to a Theravada temple whose abbot, the Venerable Sri Dhammananda, was quite influential in the Malaysian government. In the temple, the Master and the Venerable Sri Dhammananda sat in the center. The nine of us sat around the Master. Two left-home disciples of the Master and I were sitting in meditation with our eyes closed. A layman, who was a professor and a great Dharma protector of the temple, asked the Master, "Why don't the Dharma Masters of Mahayana Buddhism respect and bow to Theravada Dharma Masters?" He said a lot more that I don't remember. The Master didn't reply, and the layman kept asking. I had been meditating and not paying attention to the conversation, but for some unknown reason, I stood up and bowed to the person. I asked him, "Please tell me, before I bowed, was I a Mahayana or a Theravada Buddhist?" He couldn't answer me. A Mr. Wong, who had made the request for the Master's trip to Malaysia, told him, "He is also a professor." From then on, that layman was very kind to me and didn't ask any more questions. On that trip, every morning we would hold a small meeting to discuss what we had done the day before. The Master would sit on a high chair and we would sit on the floor. The next morning, the Master got off his chair and sat down on the floor beside me. He said, "What you did yesterday was really good!" I said, "Master, please don't praise me. I'm not afraid of anyone else's praise, because I have no attachments and I don't care. But, Master, I can't take it when you praise me. I'll be attached, because I'll be too happy." He said, "I'm not praising you. I am telling the truth." That's even worse than praising!

APPENDIX:

DISCUSSION OF
VENERABLE MASTER HSUAN HUA'S
CONTRIBUTIONS TO BUDDHISM

 beginthispart
                                                     ക   Youbing Chen

The Master traveled thousands of miles to bring the Buddhadharma to America, with the hope of establishing rules governing the Sangha that were "in accord with Dharma." For that reason sometimes the Master's instructions seemed ruthless. Sometimes they were even impossible for people to accept, for they thought the Elder Master was only capable of criticizing others. Why did they never stop to realize how hard the Master was working to try to teach and transform obstinate living beings with inferior faculties? Or how behind his stern words and tough talk was hidden so much "blood and tears." The Master said:

> I've come here prepared to teach and transform Americans. My teaching is aimed at Americans, not the Chinese people. The Chinese are incidentally gathered in.

> *Were you to ask me to go up to the heavens,*
>   *that wouldn't be hard, but teaching Americans is hard.*
> *Were you to ask me to bore into the earth,*
>   *that wouldn't be hard, but teaching Americans is hard.*
> *Were you to ask a rooster to lay an egg,*
>   *that wouldn't be hard, but teaching Americans is hard.*

From that we can realize the Master's determination to teach and transform Americans, even though it was going to be an extremely difficult task. However, the Master did it. He has a record of creating an American Sangha and of establishing Way-places that accord with Dharma and rules for governing the Sangha.

Those who knew the Venerable Master are aware that throughout his whole life he strictly upheld "taking only one meal at noon and not lying down at night," and that he put into practice the Six Guiding Principles. Especially in the turmoil of the Dharma-ending Age, the Venerable Master was even more a sure sign of the Proper Dharma and a light for living beings. The Master did not fear the slander of demons; everywhere he went he advocated the *Shurangama Sutra,* proclaiming the Proper Dharma to destroy the deviant and manifest the proper. Although during the Dharma Ending Age there are a lot of cases of "mistaking fish eyes for pearls" even within Buddhism, still, the Master's vow-power was decisive:

> I am definitely going to revive the Proper Dharma. I will only allow Buddhism to have Proper Dharma and will not let there be any demise of the Dharma. Wherever I go, that place will have blessings and wisdom and there will be a diminishing of disasters. That is my vow. Because of that, ignoring the limits of my capabilities, I go everywhere speaking the Proper Dharma and practicing the Proper Dharma.

The Master painfully remarked:

> *When the Dharma becomes extinct, it is the Sangha itself*
> *   that becomes extinct.*
> *Virtue in the Way should be cultivated, but people won't cultivate it.*
> *Those who are honest and sincere are ridiculed.*

Those who are false and cunning receive praise and precedence.
The whole world is full of five turbidities; it's rare to find any purity
Beings are made drunk by the three poisons and one knows not
when they'll wake up
Earnestly remind the young Sanghans that the flourishing of
Buddhism depends on the Bhikshus.

In Buddhism there can't be just 99 percent. If even one part of Buddhism is false, then it is no longer "Proper Dharma." And so we must distinguish clearly, because in temples there are both "deviant dharmas and externalists"—and that's no exaggeration. (The *Shurangama Sutra* said so long ago.) There are even the ones who "call themselves teachers and make themselves patriarchs," whose transmissions are "tainted Buddhism," secretly advertising their own private brand of "talismans and incantations, secret dharmas, and mudras." The Master gave instruction about this early on:

You should recognize this Way-place—you should not
fail to believe in it. Where there are Buddhas, there are
also demons. That demon has come to make trouble in
the Way-place. He's come deliberately to create chaos.

There's a saying in Buddhism: "I would rather not get rebirth for a thousand years than to enter the paths of demons for a single day." This is especially applicable to Taiwan where religion is "flourishing extraordinarily"—you can find religious professionals who are "Great Masters, Superior Masters, Unsurpassed Masters, Contemporary Buddhas, Living Buddhas, and Honored Masters" everywhere you go. Those Masters who transmit their teachings put out "Thus Come One Buddha" advertisements and sell off the Thus Come One's "family estate." As to the likes of them, if we lack the wise vision found in the "Four Clear Instructions on Purity," it's to be feared we will never be able to get out of the clutches of those "Superior Masters," but will become part of their retinue until finally we end up:

Then both the disciples and the teacher get in trouble with the law and fall into the unintermittent hells. Once a disciple made this inquiry, "The Master often says: *Truly recognize your own faults. Don't discuss the faults of others. Others' faults are just my own. To be one with everyone is called Great Compassion.* And so why is the Master always openly criticizing others in the Buddhist journal, *Vajra Bodhi Sea*? Isn't that a case of saying one thing and doing another? The Master answered:

> The one who will fall into the hells is me, not you. If what I say is true, then it's not gossip; if it's not true, then I will definitely fall into the hells. If someone says great cultivators are not subject to cause and effect, then the retribution for that is 500 lives as a fox. If I deny cause and effect—calling black white and white black, calling right wrong and wrong right—saying things that are not so, then I will go into the Hell of Pulling Tongues. If I haven't spoken incorrectly, then I have no offense. Mencius said: "I don't like to debate, but I have no choice...if the teachings of the Yang School and the Mo School aren't put to rest, then the teachings of Confucius cannot prevail. "Why do I like to talk about what's right and what's wrong? It's because in Buddhism there are entirely too many rights and wrongs! There's the black teaching, the white teaching, the yellow teaching, the red teaching—they've become all kinds of different colors that confuse the eye. It's gotten to the point that the blacks don't know they are black and the whites don't know they are white. And so I like to say things that others don't dare to say. If any of you are offended, it doesn't matter—I'm not concerned. I specialize in

breaking through people's deviant knowledge and deviant views.

From the above passage we can recognize the depth of the Master's compassionate mind, which couldn't bear to see living beings suffer. The so-called great kindness and compassion that borders on being harsh is actually an expedient used to teach and transform living beings. The Master once wrote a verse that clarifies his determination:

> I am going to speak the truth
> And I'm not afraid of being beaten or scolded.
> Kill me, I have no fear.
> What inhibitions are there in liberation?

The Master repeated his instructions about protecting and supporting the Proper Dharma many times:

> In Buddhism all the sutras are very important, but the *Shurangama Sutra* is even more important. Wherever the *Shurangama Sutra* is, the Proper Dharma abides in the world. When the *Shurangama Sutra* is gone, that is a sign of the Dharma Ending Age. In the *Extinction of the Dharma Sutra* it says that in the Dharma Ending Age, the *Shurangama Sutra* will become extinct first. Then gradually the other sutras will also become extinct. The *Shurangama Sutra* is the true body of the Buddha; the sharira of the Buddha; the stupa of the Buddha. If the *Shurangama Sutra* is false, then I am willing to fall into the unintermittent hell, stay there forever, and never again come back to the world to see all of you.

Whoever can memorize the *Shurangama Sutra*, whoever can memorize the Shurangama Mantra, is a true disciple of the Buddha.

There's no such thing as Proper, Image, or Ending Dharma ages; it's the minds of beings that have the concept of Proper, Image, and Ending. The Master considers that any time people work hard at cultivation is a time when the Proper Dharma abides. If no one cultivates, if no one reads, recites, and memorizes the *Shurangama Sutra*, then that's the Dharma Ending Age. That's because the *Shurangama Sutra's* "Four Clear Instructions on Purity" that discuss killing, stealing, lust, and lying and its "Fifty Skandha Demon-States" that expose the very bones of all the heavenly demons and externalists, both say flat out that when people don't hold the precepts, then that's the Dharma Ending Age; whenever there are precepts, there is Buddhadharma.

In 1990, in a serious talk given at the Labor Hall in Kaohsiung, Taiwan, the Master said that the Dharma Ending Age results from the laity singling out individual left-home people to protect and support. What did he mean? The Master said:

> Left-home people go off to live alone in their own temples
> and act like kings, like dictators, like emperors. The laity
> lack the "Dharma-selecting eye" and go about protecting
> here and protecting there until they protect people right
> into the hells. In the Proper Dharma Age, everyone lives
> together in large monastic complexes and cultivates
> together. In the Dharma Ending Age no one wants to
> live in large monastic complexes. It's one person per
> temple. You have your way of doing things and I have
> mine. And this throws the laity into a real quandary.
> They see that a certain monk is good-looking and decide
> to support his Dharma, so they set him up with his
> own temple. Then they notice another monk who's not
> bad and build a temple for him. Supporting this way

and supporting that way, they cause the left-home people
to get greedy for benefits to the point that they return
to lay life.

I hope Buddhism will take these words to heart and not continue to "plug up its ears while stealing a bell"—cheating all of humankind. At present the signs of turmoil in Buddhism in Taiwan are alarmingly serious. But no one dares to stand up and shout. Everyone just stands by and watches while Buddhist followers race toward their demise. Three steps and a hermitage; five steps and a big temple—they run around having Dharma Assemblies, crossing over souls, anointing crowns, transmitting dharmas, and setting up temples. They never stop to realize that they should be propagating the teachings and explaining their meanings—instructing and guiding living beings in how to end birth and death. The fundamental intent of the Buddha's teaching is education—to cause everyone to develop wisdom and the Dharma-selecting eye, so that they recognize cause and effect, cut off evil, and do good. The intent is not to focus on building monasteries and setting up temples. One wonders how much blood, sweat, and tears are hidden behind this stern instruction by the Master. As it's said, such a one "only wants the light of the torch he's holding to shine as far as possible; he's never concerned about getting burned." "Despite the odds, I will stick to my intentions." This is the best description of the Master.

In the past, Buddhism in China always gave people the mistaken impression that it was a religion that specialized in crossing over dead souls and so the intelligent looked down on and tried to get rid of Buddhism. Two years prior to the Master's Nirvana, he cried out in dispair:

Chinese Buddhism's Water Lands, Flaming Mouths, and
other ceremonies and their saving of souls have become

the "status quo" in Chinese Buddhism. They never stop to think that if they keep it up, they are going to be doing nothing but handing out free meals to unemployed vagrants under the guise of Buddhism. What a terrible shame! All they know how to do is make money saving souls! Actually, in order to save souls, you must have a foundation in virtuous conduct. Then, not to speak of reciting mantras or reciting sutras, the single sentence "you can go to rebirth" is sufficient for a soul to be able to gain rebirth in the Land of Ultimate Bliss. For those of you who lack any virtue in the Way, who don't have any cultivation, I ask you, what's your basis for being able to save souls? What you are actually doing is running up a debt with the donor. Besides that, you are destroying the basic system of Buddhism.

Right! It's a real shame that they don't open up the Tripitaka [Buddhist Canon] with its Twelve Divisions—a precious treasury of infinite wisdom—and learn to teach from it instead of applying all their effort to superfluous things.

Among Asian Buddhists who have taken refuge there is a popular misconception. Everyone thinks that the more teachers you take refuge with, the better. This is a sign of the Dharma Ending Age. By taking refuge with this one and then taking refuge with that one, they cause contention among the Dharma Masters, who quarrel with each other over who has the Dharma affinities and who gets the disciples. But the Master always asked those who had already taken refuge not to sign up to take refuge again—that they could just follow along and rejoice from the sidelines. The Master said:

Some people say, "The Youth Good Wealth visited fifty-three teachers; why can't I bow to a few more teachers?" But you need to realize that the Youth Good Wealth was always sent on by his previous teacher to the next teacher. It wasn't that he greedily longed for another Dharma Master endowed with virtuous conduct and so turned his back on his current teacher and stole away to take refuge with another. A lot of older Chinese Buddhist disciples have taken refuge tens or hundreds of times. But when you ask them what "taking refuge" means, they don't know. Isn't that pathetic? They say that all left-home people are their teachers. But I say they don't have any teacher at all because their minds lack faith, so how can they be saved?

Actually when it comes to the question of red envelopes, all along the Master was very opposed to the custom. That's because there's an element of cheating in it. No one knows how much money is in those red envelopes. For Buddhist disciples in Asia, taking refuge and red envelopes amount to the same thing. That being the case, people who can't come up with red envelopes and those of externalist ways don't dare believe in the Buddha and take refuge. The Master said:

> In the *Avatamsaka Sutra,* the Youth Good Wealth holds a very important position and yet he has had a very complicated influence on Chinese Buddhism. Most Dharma Masters know very well that for one person to take refuge with lots of different teachers is incorrect. It is not in accord with the Buddhadharma. But if they don't let it happen, their "tokens" (the red envelopes)

132

will diminish significantly. And so to this day no one
openly opposes this custom. Knowing full well it is
wrong, they still do it. Complicated, huh? Why? First,
it's for the sake of the "youths" (the laity that get pulled
in) and second it's for the sake of "Good Wealth" (one's
share of red envelopes). This is the worst habit going in
Buddhism.

The Master's true knowledge and brilliant views are decisively different
from those of the multitudes. How much compassion there is behind the
Master's lion's roar that he emits because he "cannot bear to watch the
sagely teachings decline"! A lot of "star teachers" in Taiwan, being put on
pedestals by their disciples, forget all about their responsibility to "carry on
the Thus Come One's work of saving living beings." Every day they wallow
in their intoxication with fame and profit and neglect the great matter of
birth and death. Actually when disciples of the Triple Jewel encounter left-
home teachers, they should inquire about the Buddhadharma, not just be
intent upon giving them red envelopes. That's why the Master encouraged
his disciples to hold the precept against possessing money as much as possible;
to avoid "tying up conditions" with money as much as possible. The Master
said:

> That's because left-home people can cultivate if they
> don't have money. As soon as they have money, then
> they certainly won't be able to cultivate. I can guarantee
> it. Look into it! Investigate it. Taoists are referred to as
> "poor Taoists." Sanghans are referred to as "poor
> Sanghans." Nobody talks about "rich Sanghans" or "rich
> Taoists." And so when you use your money to make
> offerings to "rich Sanghans" and "rich Taoists," it's the

same as if you were committing offenses. I'm going to offend a lot of people by saying this. But although I am offending you, I still have to tell the truth.

Everyone knows that "wearing the precept sash and eating one meal a day" are the tradition of the City of Ten Thousand Buddhas. The Master specifically announced that anyone who left home with him had to honor the Buddha's regulations of eating one meal a day at noon and always wearing the precept sash. And so no matter how must the City of Ten Thousand Buddhas came under criticism by those outside—even when people slandered the City as doing new and strange things to show off, the Master would never, ever change his policy because of that. Regarding the barrage of slander, the Master merely said: "This is not some rule I made up. This is the Buddha's regulation. We want to honor the Buddha's regulations." But the Master was expedient with the older left-home people and allowed them to take three meals a day. This rule remained right up to the final instructions given by the Master just before his Nirvana—it never changed. The Master himself said:

> If people who want to leave home with me can eat one meal a day, then I will accept them. If they cannot eat one meal a day, I will not accept them. This is a fixed requirement for anyone who leaves home with me. In spite of any pressures whatsoever regarding the times and circumstances, this cannot be changed.
>
> I'm prepared to die, if you want, but I refuse not to wear my precept sash. I'm prepared to die, if you want, but I refuse not to eat only once a day at noon. Those who have that kind of strong samadhi-power—that kind

of faith—rightfully belong at the City of Ten Thousand Buddhas.

Some people look at it this way: "This is not the time of the Buddha and we are not in India now; what is more Chinese people are not Indians, and so, since the precepts were created for the times, the locations and the people, then they are precepts only applicable to the people of India and are not appropriate for the people of China." Actually that is incorrect because the precepts are one of the three non-outflow studies of precepts, samadhi, and wisdom in Buddhism, all of which were explained by Shakyamuni Buddha himself. If "precepts" are not appropriate to the people of China, then does that mean that "samadhi and wisdom" are also not appropriate to the people of China? Ridiculous!

The Master sternly insisted that those who left-home under him absolutely must wear the sash at all times—the precept sash must never leave their bodies. The Master said,

> For left-home people not to wear their precept sashes is the same as going back to lay-life. You are no different from ordinary people. It's not that wearing the long robe that fastens on the side proves that you are a left-home person. Not to speak of just wearing the long robe—even when you wear your precept sash—all you do every day is violate the precepts and be dishonest, how much the more so when you don't wear your sash!
>
> Chinese left-home people of today, even the left-home people of other countries as well—the majority of Great Vehicle Buddhists—do not wear their precept sashes. They think that's the status quo—the way things are

supposed to be. What they don't realize is that as soon
as they don't wear their precept sashes, they lose the
appearance of Bhikshus.

The Master decisively thinks that left-home people absolutely must wear
their precept sashes, otherwise they don't have the semblance of being
Bhikshus. Besides, wearing the sash is the trademark of Buddhist disciples.
The Buddha himself had three robes (sashes), a bowl, and a sitting cloth,
and his robe (sash) never left his body. This was mentioned in the
Compilation of Dharanis Sutra where it says: "The Buddha's body was the
color of true gold and he was wearing a saffron *kashaya.*" Also the *Essentials
Regarding Recitation Sutra* says: "The Buddha's body, like azure, is endowed
with thirty-two hallmarks and eighty subtle characteristics. He is wearing
a saffron kashaya and is seated in full lotus posture." We can see that the
Master is not unreasonable in advocating wearing the precept sash.

The Sutras which the Master lectured during his life are generally listed
here: *Avatamsaka Sutra, Dharma Flower Sutra, Shurangama Sutra*—more
than thirty different ones. Also among the Chinese classics he lectured: *The
Four Books,* the *Book of Changes,* and the *Nature of Chinese Medicine.* Among
all these are three that are quite unusual—very few people have ever explained
them. They are: *Verses and Commentary on the Shurangama Mantra, Reflections
in Water and Mirrors Turning Back the Tide of Destiny,* and modern-language
explanations of the *Biographies of the Buddhist Patriarchs.*

The Master' lecture series on *Verses and Commentary on the Shurangama
Mantra* lasted for eight years, from 1979 to 1987. Throughout all of Buddhist
history this mantra has rarely been explained. Only Great Master Xu Fa of
the Qing dynasty and Dharma Master Bo Ting of Compassionate Cloud
Monastery in Wulin ever explained it. When the Master came in possession
of a copy of the *Commentary on the Shurangama Mantra* in 1949, he records:

I obtained what I'd never had before. I got a glimpse of the state of the esoteric, carrying it always with me and never being apart from it.

He also said:

For the Proper Dharma to remain long in the world, and to stop the deviant discourses once and for all, everyone should carry a copy, and we should enter the ultimately firm great samadhi together.

Later, after the Master came to America, he himself explained the Shurangama Mantra, writing verses of seven-character lines to explain each of the 554 lines and further giving a modern-language commentary. Truly this masterpiece is unprecedented. It is exceptionally valuable. The Master said:

The four-line verses used to explain every line of the mantra don't by any means exhaust the meaning, because the wonderful meanings in the mantra are infinite and endless. These four-line verses are a mere mention of the broad idea—just tendering a bit of brick, hoping someone will come up with jade. These four-line verse appear to be very simple, but they flow out from my heart. You could say they are my blood and sweat. They certainly aren't plagiarized—copied from someone else's work!.....

I'm explaining the Shurangama Mantra for you now, and thoroughout hundreds of thousands of eons, no one even explains it once. Also, it's not easy to explain in its entirety. When I'm explaining it, I know that none of you really understand what I'm saying. Even if there are those who think they do, they don't really. But perhaps ten years from now, or a hundred, or a thousand years from now, someone will read this simple explanation and gain a profound understanding of the mantra.

Reflections in Water and Mirrors Turning Back the Tide of Destiny is a series of essays composed and explained by the Master during the four-year period from 1985 to 1989. It includes praises and objective critiques of Buddhas, Bodhisattvas, Arhats, lofty Sanghans of great virtue, Buddhist lay persons, men and women of great virtue throughout history both in and outside of China, remarkable individuals, national leaders, literati, and so on. Just as Confucius compiled the *Spring and Autumn Annals*, the Master wrote *Water and Mirrors* out of his patriotic loyalty and his wish to save the world from impending chaos and turmoil. We could alter Confucius' quote to fit the Master: "If people understand me, it is because of *Water and Mirrors*; if people blame me, it is also because of *Water and Mirrors*." *Water and Mirrors* carries on the spirit and intent of *Spring and Autumn Annals*, and is a living record of causes and effects as they occur in the world today. After giving a brief biographical sketch of each person, the Master praises or critiques him or her with a four-line verse of eight characters per line, and then gives another verse of seven-character lines in conclusion. This book is worth repeated reading and reflection, for it teaches us about cause and effect. Studying the past, we can know the future and be warned to stop evil and cultivate goodness.

The Master gave modern-language explanations of the *Biographies of the Buddhist Patriarchs* from 1972 to 1985. During those thirteen years, the Master delivered a total of 346 lectures on the topic. The book begins with Shakyamuni Buddha holding up a flower and smiling, transmitting the Dharma to the Venerable Kashyapa. The Dharma was then transmitted

138

to the Second Patriarch Venerable Ananda, the Third Patriarch Venerable Upali, and so on, all the way to Great Master Bodhidharma, the Twenty-eight Patriarch, who brought the Dharma of Chan to China and become the First Patriarch in China. After the time of the Thirty-third Patriarch (the Sixth Chinese Patriarch) Great Master Huineng, Buddhism divided into five sects, which later became seven sects: Fayan, Caodong, Yunmen, Weiyang, Linji, Huanglong, and Yangqi. With the addition of the Niutou branch; the Indian and Chinese Sanghans who certified to sagehood; the patriarchs of the Tiantai, Huayan, Cien, Yogacharya, Vinaya, and Lotus Society Sects; and ten contemporary eminent Sanghans [Dharma Masters Hsu Yun, Ci Zhou, Hong Yi, Tai Xu, Di Xian, Yuan Ying, Ci Hang, Tan Xu, Chang Ren, and Guang Qin], the book covers 338 people in all. The Master wrote an eight line verse (seven characters per line) in praise of each one. And for all the individuals from Great Master Yongmingshou, the Sixth Patriarch of the Lotus Sect, to the last one, Venerable Master Guang Qin, the Master wrote an additional eight line verse (four characters per line) of praise for each. With his lectures and verses, the Master provided a detailed explanation of each patriarch. The original text, in classical Chinese, devoid of punctuation, and couched in the abstruse jargon of the Chan School which is used to describe states of awakening, was extremely difficult to understand. Unable to fathom the profound states of the great cultivators of the past, one could only say they were "ineffable" or make the comment that "Only the person who drinks the water will know how hot or cold it is."

Actually there was a compelling reason for the Venerable Master to lecture on the *Biographies of the Buddhist Patriarchs*. The book was mailed to the Master in 1958 by the Venerable Elder Master Hsu Yun, who wrote in a letter,

I am sending a copy of the recently published book of prints of the Buddhist Patriarchs for you to read and keep as a remembrance. I hope that you will benefit yourself and benefit others in your work for Buddhism and that you will take care.

On the ninth of the fourth month, 1956, the Venerable Yun sent a letter to the Master making him the ninth patriarch of the Weiyang Sect. Part of the letter states:

> ...You, Venerable One, have concern for the preservation of the Dharma and for the continuation of the wisdom life of the Buddhas and Patriarchs. I am sending you the Source, the inheritance of the Patriarchs' pulse. It is my sincere hope that, entrusted to you, the Patriarchs' Way will prosper. This letter has been brief because there is no way to express all there is to say.

And so the Master followed the Elder Master's instructions, giving modern-language explanations of the *Biographies of the Buddhist Patriarchs* and benefiting living beings with this Dharma. This was an unprecedented contribution. Thus, I have considered these three works to be the Master's "three treasures." Only those with blessings have the opportunity to read such precious Dharma treasures.

Surveying the prolific verses that the Master wrote in his life, I estimate that there must be at least two thousand, each and every one of them matched and rhymed. How can we not admire the Master's profound Prajna wisdom? To explain the Shurangama Mantra in verses is an unprecedented achievement. How could he have done this if he had not entered the esoteric realm of the Great Shurangama Samadhi? Moreover, the Master's explanations of the *Biographies of the Buddhist Patriarchs* sometimes went beyond the documented historical records, making us suspect that he really did have the power of knowing past lives.

The Master vowed,

> As long as I have a breath left, I will expound the Sutras
> and speak the Dharma.

That is why he composed so prolifically. His vow to translate the Buddhist canon into the languages of the world will generate infinite and boundless merit and virtue. The Dharma Realm Buddhist Association has already published over a hundred volumes of translations of Sutras and Dharma talks. After the Master's passing, the work of canonical translation will continue without interruption, eternally leading living beings from darkness into the light, from this shore of suffering to the other shore of ultimate Nirvana.

If we survey the Master's teachings and conduct, we find that they carry the flavor of Lao Zi's philosophy. In his verse on Venerable Mahakashyapa in *Water and Mirrors*, the Master says,

> *Transforming himself, he appeared as Lao Zi and wandered*
> *throughout China,*
> *Guiding those with affinities to ascend to the other shore.*

Clearly the Master considered Lao Zi a transformation body of Venerable Mahakashyapa. Lao Zi's one and only 5000-word composition became widely popular among the people and cultivators of China. Many of the Master's words and deeds bear a striking resemblance to those of Lao Zi. For example, Lao Zi said:

> Straightforward words seem paradoxical.
> Truthful words are not beautiful; beautiful words are not true.

> Turning back is how the Way moves;
> Yielding is the means the Way employs.

The Master often used contrary teachings to stimulate people. For example, when someone asked whether it would be permissible to kill small insects in the household, the Master replied,

> If you want to kill little insects, you must kill me first!

How compassionate the Master was! The Master always taught living beings the Six Guiding Principles (equivalent to the five precepts): no fighting, no greed, no seeking, no selfishness, no pursuit of personal benefit, and no lying. Many people were unconvinced, wondering why the Master bothered to lecture on principles that any three-year-old could understand. Yet the Master said over and over,

> Everything I have accomplished in this life came from practicing the Six Guiding Principles. If any of you want to cultivate the path to Buddhahood, you also must practice the Six Guiding Principles.

Lao Zi himself also said:

> My words are very easy to understand and very easy to put into practice, yet no one in the world can understand them or put them into practice.

> The great Way is easy, yet people prefer by-paths.

Cultivation is basically a very simple affair. "The Way is near; don't seek it afar." Yet people like to take shortcuts, to visit various teachers in search of "secret dharmas" to cultivate. "Indeed, it is long since the people were perplexed." Little do they know that the secret is within them: if they can stop pursuing material pleasures, let go of discriminations and attachments, and refrain from anger and lying, then that's the "secret dharma" and the Way right there! Having awakened to the Six Guiding Principles after a lifetime of bitter cultivation, the Master fervently wished to offer them to the world for the benefit of living beings. Yet people paid no attention to them, and even snorted and laughed at them. It is exactly as Lao Zi said:

> When the best student hears about the Way,
> He practices it assiduously;
> When the average student hears about the Way,
> It seems to him one moment there and gone the next;
> When the worst student hears about the Way
> He laughs out loud.
> If he did not laugh,
> It would be unworthy of being the Way.

The Master's lifelong philosophy of noncontention is the same as Lao Zi's. People who truly do not contend have no anger. They forgive people whenever it is possible to forgive them. The Master wrote these verses:

> Fighting involves the thought of winning and losing
> And so it goes against the Way.
> Giving rise to the mind of the four marks,
> How can you obtain samadhi?

> All things easily come and go,
> But a bad temper's truly hard to change.
> If you can really never get angry,
> Then you've found a precious jewel.

> When you stop putting the blame on others,
> Then everything goes your way.
> If you never let your mind get afflicted,
> Then the karma born of hatred won't return to trouble you.
> But whoever dwells on others' faults
> Simply proves that his own suffering hasn't reached an end.

Aside from the Six Guiding Principles, the Master gave us two other verses that are worth remembering and practicing for the rest of our lives:

Truly recognize your own faults,
Don't discuss the faults of others.
Others' faults are just my own.
Being one with everyone is great compassion.

Everything's a test
To see what you will do.
If you don't recognize what's before you,
You'll have to start anew.

In the *Analects* and the *Mencius*, we can read the teachings of sages: "If you fail in your endeavor, look for the reason in yourself." The Master also taught people to seek within themselves, and his teachings sometimes caught them off guard. For example, on February 10, 1993, the Master appeared wearing a veil over his face at the City of Ten Thousand Buddhas because his disciples had broken the rules of eating only one meal a day and always wearing the sash. He said,

> Even before I went to Taiwan, I knew that all the principles I had laid down since the founding of the City of Ten Thousand Buddhas were completely gone, no longer being followed. That's why I am terribly disappointed and feel I have no face with which to see you...I have to wear a veil so that I will not see you with my naked face.

That was the first time in Buddhist history that a teacher had veiled his face before his disciples in order to hide his shame. Actually, we who broke the precepts are the ones who should have veiled our faces, not the Master. In the spring of 1992, the City of Ten Thousand Buddhas held an unprecedented Unrestrained Repentance Assembly (for details see issues 261-265 of *Vajra Bodhi Sea*), during which the Master said:

> I gave myself several painful beatings until I nearly fainted, because due to my lack of virtue, the disciples I taught turned out to be like this.
>
> If your repentance is sincere, then no matter what mistakes you have made, I can be responsible for them. But if you refuse to tell the truth and you want to fall to the hells faster, then I have no way to save you.

I know of no other teacher who beats himself when his disciples are disobedient. It really shakes me up and makes me feel bad. The Master's actual practice of the philosophy that "Others' faults are just my own; / To be one with everyone is great compassion" is very obvious. It is just as Chapter Twenty-five of the *Flower Adornment Sutra* says:

> I should undergo every suffering for the sake of all living beings, enabling them to escape the great pit of limitless births and deaths. I should, for the sake of all living beings in all of the evil destinies in all worlds, undergo all sufferings to the end of time... I wish to undergo the sufferings of such living beings myself so that they do not have to fall into the hells. When they are in the hells, the animal realm, King Yama's court, or other dangerous places, I shall give up my own body to ransom them and enable them to gain liberation from the evil paths.

Confucius said in the *Analects*: "He who makes liberal demands upon himself

and small demands on others, will keep resentment far from himself."
(Chapter Fifteen "Weilinggong") King Tang of the Shang dynasty made a
sacrifice and appealed to heaven, saying, "If I have offenses, the people are
not to blame. If the people have offenses, the blame rests with me." The
words, deeds, and teachings of the sages are all the same. The only way to
influence others is to set an example for them and subdue oneself. The
Master once wrote a verse:

> With vast, proper energy suffusing the universe,
> Achieve greatness and transform it, learning from the sages.
> When you fail, look within yourself.
> Turn the light around and illumine within; don't exploit situations.
>
> Act like an old fool; don't be too clever.
> Diligently sweep the dust from the mind, get rid of selfish treachery.
> If you can constantly urge yourself on in this way,
> The Buddhadharma will soon fill the trichiliocosm.

Finally, let's discuss the Master's philosophy of kowtowing. The Master
once remarked that the secret of his lifelong cultivation consisted of
kowtowing to others and taking losses. The Master often exhorted new
disciples who had just taken refuge with him:

> If someone scolds me, you should bow to him. No
> matter who slanders me, never speak in my defense.

In America the Master often bowed to his disciples. Whenever he bowed to
disobedient disciples, they became obedient. In the early days in America,
one evening when the Master was lecturing on a Sutra at Wonderful Words
Hall in the City of Ten Thousand Buddhas, none of his left-home disciples
would go up on stage and speak. After the lecture, when everyone was
leaving Wonderful Words Hall to return to the Buddha hall, the Master
knelt by the door and watched as the entire assembly walked out. His stern

self-castigation was a wordless teaching to all. It was truly an example of Space Age cultivation. The fact that he could kowtow to his disciples proves that he had realized the state of egolessness. When the Master invited other Dharma Masters to lecture at the City, he personally led the assembly in kneeling to listen to the lecture. He certainly was not arrogant as some people have described him.

Many contemporary Buddhist scholars only know to bow to the Buddha outside; they do not know to bow to the Buddha in their own mind. Nor do they know to admit their mistakes before their parents and all living beings. Thus their practice is not complete. We should learn to bow and repent daily before our parents and all living beings. We should constantly seek within ourselves, reflect upon ourselves, and listen to our own nature. Seeing worthy ones, we should strive to emulate them. Seeing unworthy ones, we should examine our own faults.

The ultimate goal of studying Buddhism is to put an end to birth and death. There is an ancient saying:

> *If love is not cut off, one cannot be born in the*
> *Land of Ultimate Bliss.*
> *If one's offenses weren't grave, one would not have been born*
> *in the Saha world.*

If we do not eliminate emotional desires, there is no way we can end birth and death. The *Shurangama Sutra* says: "If you don't renounce your lustful thoughts, you will not be able to get out of the dust." "If living beings in the six paths of any mundane world had no thoughts of lust, they would not have to follow a continual succession of births and deaths." Lustful desire is the fundamental root of birth and death. That's why the Master always spoke out against sexual misconduct and lustful desire. Even up to the year before he entered the stillness, he continued to repeat:

People are born because of lust and die because of lust.
That's all there is to it.

The Master said the City of Ten Thousand Buddhas is very old-fashioned in that boys and girls study in separate schools. The purpose of this is to encourage everyone to follow the rules and not engage in sexual misconduct, not have abortions, and not take birth control pills; lust is the primary reason the world has gone bad. The Master said:

> Boys should wait until after they are twenty-five to look for a girlfriend; girls should wait until after they are twenty to look for a boyfriend.

> If you cannot cut off love and desire, then even if you are a monk or nun for eighty thousand great eons, you are merely wasting your time in Buddhism and creating karma with every meal you take.

Today's newspapers are filled with reports of murder, robbery, lust, and fraud, with the incidences of murder and lust being especially high. The Master said:

> In terms of cause and effect, sexual misconduct is the gravest offense, and those who engage in it are punished very severely. According to the law of cause and effect, however many times a person commits adultery, after death he or she will be sawed from head to foot that many times by a huge saw. If they were married a hundred times in life, they will be divided into a hundred parts after death.

Great Master Yin Guang spoke very sternly with regard to sexual misconduct:

Those who engage in sexual misconduct have no shame or modesty and are filthy and evil to the extreme. Although they have human bodies, they conduct themselves like animals and become animals in this very life. In their next life they will be reborn as animals... Those who engage in sexual misconduct will have children who do not preserve chastity... Those who engage in masturbation, even if they engage in no other form of sexual misconduct, will fall into the great hells. After leaving the hells, they will be reborn as female pigs or female dogs. If they are born among humans, they will be prostitutes...

Some people may wonder if the patriarchs' instructions are blowing things out of proportion or going to far to the other extreme in trying to correct the trend. Actually, living beings in the Dharma-ending Age have committed so much evil that if they didn't "go too far," they wouldn't be able to correct the trend. The patriarchs have their reasons for giving such instructions, and we need not entertain doubts or speculations. As Lao Zi said, "Straightforward words seem paradoxical."

In the numerous question-answer exchanges between the Master and those in the audience, the Master's unexpected answers often caught people off guard and filled them with the joy of Dharma, evoking cheers and rounds of applause. His humorous answers, fraught with hidden Chan meanings, always hit right on the mark and pointed straight at the mind. Let us quote a passage from Chapter Eight "Sudden and Gradual" of the *Sixth Patriarch Sutra* to shed light on the Master's Prajna humor:

Those who see their own nature can establish dharmas in their minds or not establish them as they choose.

> They come and go freely, without impediments or obstacles. They function correctly and speak appropriately, seeing all transformation bodies as integral with the self-nature. That is precisely the way they obtain independence, spiritual powers, and the samadhi of playfulness. This is what is called seeing the nature.

The meaning of this passage is that people of genuine enlightenment who have understood the mind and seen the nature can establish methods or not establish them. They come and go without obstruction. They have freedom over life and death. If someone asks them a question, they can answer without thinking, but their answers have principle. They don't speak recklessly. They see transformation bodies everywhere, but these transformation bodies are within the self-nature. At all times they contemplate with independence and have the five eyes and six spiritual powers. People who have seen their nature can answer spontaneously without fear of answering wrong and misleading others. Below are some of the Master's answers to questions asked by the audience:

> If no one has blessed ("opened the light on") a Buddha image, can we bow to it?
>
> **Answer:** If your mind is free of attachments, the Buddha image is always blessed. If your mind is attached, then even if it is blessed, it just the same as if it hadn't been blessed.

> How can we avoid an earthquake?
>
> **Answer:** If no one gets angry, there won't be any earthquakes.
>
> How can I end birth and death?
>
> **Answer:** Eat, dress, and sleep.

What Sutra or mantra should we recite that will make it easiest to become a Buddha?

Answer: Recite the Sutra of not getting angry, the Sutra of not scolding others, and the Sutra of not losing your temper. With these three Sutras, you'll become a Buddha real soon!

How can we cut off lust?

Answer: Don't think about it, and you will have cut it off! If you keep thinking about it, how can you cut it off? Be aware of each thought as soon as it arises; once you are aware of it, it goes away.

Dharma Master, where will you go after you enter perfect stillness?

Answer: Nowhere at all!

How can we break through attachments and random thoughts?

Answer: Who gave you attachments? Who gave you random thoughts?

How can we "produce the thought which is nowhere supported"?

Answer: Where is your mind? First tell me that.

Ultimately, is it people who fear ghosts or ghosts who fear people?

Answer: If you have ghosts in your mind, then people fear ghosts. If there are no ghosts in your mind, then ghosts fear people.

How can we secure rebirth?

Answer: Why do you want to be reborn? How can you make it when you're dragging so much junk around?

Someone once said to the Master, "It makes me feel so bad to see the Master using a walking cane and taking on so much karma for living beings. I hope the Master will be compassionate and live a long time." The Venerable Master immediately flung his cane aside, evoking a round of applause, and asked, "Do you feel better now?" This was the Master's wonderful Prajna of being able to "leave all appearances while in the midst of appearances." Don't you find this thought-provoking? Throughout his entire life, the Master emphasized "not getting angry" and "being patient with insult," because "The Buddhadharma is here in the world; / Enlightenment is not apart from the world. / To search for Bodhi apart from the world / Is like looking for a hare with horns." The Master said: "If a person can refrain from losing his temper, all his karmic obstacles will be cancelled at once." It is interesting to note two famous mantras that the Master composed:

> *Patience, patience, gotta have patience.*
> *Don't get angry, suo po he!*
>
> *Purge the fire in your liver,*
> *And you'll be free from all illness.*
> *What a shame this wonderful elixir*
> *Gets stored away and forgotten altogether!*
> *Suo po he.*

If we read the Master's talks and answers to questions with careful attention, they will easily activate the wisdom inherent in our natures. As it is said, "General summaries and detailed explanations all express truth in the primary sense." As the Master often said,

> You don't have to believe in me or believe in the Buddha.
> Believe in your own inherent wisdom. Discover the

> Prajna in your own nature. Then you'll attain Dharma-
> selecting Vision. You'll know to advance upon the Way
> and to retreat from what is not the Way. Don't wear
> your hat like a shoe.

The five eyes and six spiritual powers discussed in Buddhism are merely manifestations of Prajna that occur as we cultivate towards the goal of attaining freedom from outflows and becoming enlightened. They are not to be regarded as extraordinary. In order to avoid falling into deviant paths, we should uphold the precepts purely and keep our minds free from greed and defilement. Actually, spiritual powers are merely powers inherent in our own natures. Everyone is endowed with the Buddha nature, and so everyone possesses the five eyes and six spiritual powers. It is just that they have been covered by our ignorance and afflictions. The Buddha warned people not to casually reveal their spiritual powers, but he didn't absolutely forbid it. If a Bodhisattva has spiritual powers but does not use them expediently to teach living beings, then what's the use of having them? The chapter "The Merit and Virtue of Bringing forth the Mind" in the *Flower Adornment Sutra* says, "Dwelling in the ultimate path of the One Vehicle, deeply entering the wondrous and supreme Dharma, knowing well when living beings are ready and when they are not, he manifests spiritual powers in order to benefit them."

Many people mistakenly view the Master as someone who showed off his spiritual powers. Yet, going through the Master's instructional talks and taped lectures, I have yet to find an instance in which the Master acknowledged that he had spiritual powers. The Master said:

> I'm telling you the truth: I don't have spiritual powers;
> I don't even have ghostly powers. I hope people will not
> exaggerate the facts and stretch the truth.

If you knew the Master only as someone who had spiritual powers, it's a great pity, for you were not truly his disciple. I knew the Master not as someone who possessed the five eyes and six spiritual powers, but as an elder who was truly compassionate and selfless. I knew him as a teacher who painfully hit himself with his own cane, who begged for and confiscated people's bad tempers, who fasted for world peace, who traveled everywhere speaking Dharma even when confined to a wheelchair, and who prostrated himself to living beings every day. He was someone who spared no blood or sweat and never paused to rest as he practiced the Bodhisattva Way.

If a Buddhist knows only whether his teacher has special powers but does not understand his teacher's attitude and compassion in teaching beings, he has confounded what is important with what is trivial; he is not a true Buddhist disciple.

The Master spoke of how he came alone from Asia to America, a land where Buddhism was virtually unknown, with the sole purpose of bringing the Orthodox Dharma to the West. The City of Ten Thousand Buddhas has now become the most important Buddhist monastic complex in the West, and there are various branch monasteries as well. Leading his disciples at the City of Ten Thousand Buddhas and other places, the Master tread the long, hard road with steady and determined footsteps, working to propagate the Proper Dharma and to unite all religions. The Master vowed that all living beings had to become Buddhas before he would do so; he wanted to help all living beings to escape suffering and attain bliss, and to discover true wisdom, comfort, and liberation. The Master said:

> I am a little ant that wishes to walk beneath the feet of all Buddhists; I am a road that all living beings can traverse from the state of ordinary people to Buddhahood.

> If any disciple of mine falls into the hells, I am willing
> to stand in for them. May anyone who sees me, hears
> my voice, or even hears my name quickly attain
> Buddhahood. I'm willing to wait in the Saha world until
> all of you have attained Buddhahood.

The Master's lifelong contributions to Buddhism are as vast as space itself. How could this article completely describe them? He left us countless treasures of Dharma. From today onwards, in order to repay the Master's efforts, we should increase our vigor and follow the six guiding principles in our practice. We hope the Master will soon return, based upon his vows, to cross over living beings.

THE MASTER'S INSTRUCTIONS UPON
TAKING REFUGE

Those of you who have taken refuge with me are the blood and flesh of my very own body. No matter which part of my body is cut off, it will be very painful. No matter which part of my body bleeds, my constitution will be injured. Therefore, you should all unite together. In order to cause Buddhism to flourish, you have to take the losses that others are unwilling to take and endure the insults that others are unable to endure. You must expand the measure of your mind and behave honestly. If your actions are not genuine, the Buddhas and Bodhisattvas will know. You can't deceive them. Everyone must examine his or her own faults and earnestly correct the mistakes of the past. Truly recognize your past upside-down behavior and unprincipled practices. Be honest. Forget about yourself and work for Buddhism and the entire whole of society. In this world, every organization and every society has its own complications and internal struggles. At Gold Mountain Monastery, the City of Ten Thousand Buddhas, Gold Wheel Monastery, and all other branch monasteries under the auspices of Dharma Realm Buddhist Association, we have to reform that kind of situation. Of course, we cannot become perfect right away, but we should work step by step to change until we reach the most perfect, most thorough, and most ultimate level. Then we have to preserve that kind of wholesome behavior and resolve in thought after thought, so that we will be able to help Buddhism expand and flourish. Every disciple should have this responsibility and think, "If the Buddhism is not prospering, that's because I have not fulfilled my responsibility." Don't shift the responsibility onto other people's shoulders. If everyone can think that way, then in the near future Buddhism will certainly be able to flourish and spread to every corner of the world!

THE EIGHTEEN GREAT VOWS OF
THE VENERABLE MASTER HUA

1.   I vow that as long as there is a single Bodhisattva in the three periods of time throughtout the ten directions of the Dharma Realm, to the very end of empty space, who has not accomplished Buddhahood. I too will not attain the right enlightenment.

2.   I vow that as long as there is a single Pratyekabuddha in the three periods of time throughout the ten directions of the Dharma Realm, to the very end of empty space, who has not accomplished Buddhahood, I too will not attain the right enlightenment.

3.   I vow that as long as there is a single Shravaka in the three periods of time throughout the ten directions of the Dharma Realm, to the very end of empty space, who has not accomplished Buddhahood, I too will not attain the right enlightenment.

4.   I vow that as long as there is a single god in the Triple Realm who has not accomplished Buddhahood, I too will not attain the right enlightenment.

5.   I vow that as long as there is a single human being in the worlds of the ten directions who has not accomplished Buddhahood, I too will not attain the right enlightenment.

6.   I vow that as long as there is a single asura who has not accomplished Buddhahood, I too will not attain the right enlightenment.

7.   I vow that as long as there is a single animal who has not accomplished Buddhahood, I too will not attain the right enlightenment.

8.   I vow that as long as there is a single hungry ghost who has not accomplished Buddhahood, I too will not attain the right enlightenment.

9.   I vow that as long as there is a single hell-dweller who has not accomplished Buddhahood, I too will not attain the right enlightenment.

10.   I vow that as long as there is a single god, immortal, human, asura, air-bound or water-bound creature, animate or inanimate object, or a single dragon, beast, ghost, or spirit, ets., of the spiritual realm that has taken refuge with me and has not accomplished Buddhahood, I too will not attain the right enlightenment.

11.   I vow to fully dedicate all blessings and bliss which I ought myself receive and enjoy to all living beings of the Dharma Realm.

12.   I vow to fully take upon myself all sufferings and hardships of all the living beings in the Dharma Realm.

13.   I vow to manifest innumerable bodies as a means to gain access into the minds of living beings throughout the universe who do not believe in the Buddhadharma, causing them to correct their faults and tend toward wholesomeness, repent of their errors and start anew, take refuge in the Triple Jewel, and ultimately accomplish Buddhahood.

14.   I vow that all living beings who see my face or even hear my name will fix their thoughts on Bodhi and quickly accomplish the Buddha Way.

15.   I vow to respectfully observe the Buddha's instructions and cultivate the practice of eating only one meal per day.

16.   I vow to enlighten all sentient beings, universally responding to the multitude of differing potentials.

17.   I vow to obtain the five eyes, six spiritual powers, and the freedom of being able to fly in this very life.

18.   I vow that all of my vows will certainly be fulfilled.

Conclusion:

> I vow to save the innumerable living beings.
> I vow to eradicate the inexhaustible afflictions
> I vow to study the illimitable Dharma-doors.
> I vow to accomplish the unsurpassed Buddha Way.

DHARMA REALM BUDDHIST
ASSOCIATION

Mission

The Dharma Realm Buddhist Association was founded by the Venerable Master Hsuan Hua in 1959. Taking the Dharma Realm as its scope, the Association aims to disseminate the genuine teachings of the Buddha throughout the world. The Association is dedicated to translating the Buddhist canon, propagating the Orthodox Dharma, promoting ethical education, and bringing benefit and happiness to all beings. Its hope is that individuals, families, the society, the nation, and the entire world will, under the transforming influence of the Buddhadharma, gradually reach the state of ultimate truth and goodness.

The Founder

The Venerable Master, whose names were An Tse and To Lun, received the Dharma name Hsuan Hua and the transmission of Dharma from Venerable Master Hsu Yun in the lineage of the Wei Yang Sect. He was born in Manchuria, China, at the beginning of the century. At nineteen, he entered the monastic order and dwelt in a hut by his mother's grave to practice filial piety. He meditated, studied the teachings, ate only one meal a day, and slept sitting up. In 1948 he went to Hong Kong, where he established the Buddhist Lecture Hall and other Way-places. In 1962, he brought the Proper Dharma to the West, lecturing on several dozen Mahayana Sutras in the United States. Over the years, the Master established more than twenty monasteries of Proper Dharma under the auspices of the Dharma Realm Buddhist Association and the City of Ten Thousand Buddhas. He also founded centers for the translation of the Buddhist canon and for education to spread the influence of the Dharma in the East and West. The Master manifested the stillness in the United States in 1995. Through his lifelong, selfless dedication to teaching living beings with wisdom and compassion, he influence countless people to change their faults and to walk upon the pure, bright path to enlightenment.

BUDDHIST TEXT TRANSLATION
PUBLICATIONS

Buddhist Sutras. Amitabha Sutra, Dharma Flower (Lotus) Sutra, Flower Adornment (Avatamsaka) Sutra, Heart Sutra & Verses without a Stand, Shurangama Sutra, Sixth Patriarch Sutra, Sutra in Forty-Two Sections, Sutra of the Past Vows of Earth Store Bodhisattva, Vajra Prajna Paramita (Diamond) Sutra.

Biographical. In Memory of the Venerable Master Hsuan Hua, Pictorial Biography of the Venerable Master Hsu Yun, Records of High Sanghans, Records of the Life of the Venerable Master Hsuan Hua, Three Steps One Bow, World Peace Gathering, News from True Cultivators, Open Your Eyes Take a Look at the World, With One Heart Bowing to the City of 10000 Buddhas.

Commentarial Literature. Buddha Root Farm, City of 10000 Buddhas Recitation Handbook, Filiality: The Human Source, Herein Lies the Treasure Trove, Listen to Yourself Think Everything Over, Shastra on the Door to Understanding the Hundred Dharmas, The Ten Dharma Realms Are Not Beyond a Single Thought, Talks on Dharma, Trip to Taiwan, Europe Talks.

Children's Book. Cherishing Life, Human Roots: Buddhist Stories for Young Readers, Giant Turtle, Bodhidharma

Musics, Novels and Brochures. Songs for Awakening, Awakening CDs', Three Cart Patriarch CDs'

The Buddhist Monthly-Vajra Bodhi Sea is a monthly journal of orthodox Buddhism which has been published by the Dharma Realm Buddhist Association. Each issue contains the most recent translations of the Buddhist canon by the Buddhist Text Translation Society. The journal is bilingual, Chinese and English.

Please visit our web-site at **www.bttsonline.org** for the latest publications.

NAMO DHARMA PROTECTOR WEI TOU BODHISATTVA

Daily Schedule at The City of Ten Thousand Buddhas

3:30 am	Wake-up
4:00 ~ 5:00 am	Morning Recitation
5:00 ~ 6:00 am	Universal Bowing
6:15 ~ 6:45 am	Breakfast for Laity
7:00 ~ 8:00 am	Avatamsaka Sutra Recitation
8:00 ~ 10:00 am	Community Work
10:30 ~ 10:45 am	Meal Offering
11:45 ~ 12:00 pm	End of Meal Offering
12:30 ~ 2:00 pm	Great Compassion Repentance
2:00 ~ 5:00 pm	Community Work
5:15 ~ 5:45 pm	Dinner for Laity
6:30 ~ 7:30 pm	Evening Recitation
7:30 ~ 9:00 pm	Lecture
9:00 ~ 9:30 pm	Heart Mantra
10:30 pm	Light Off

DHARMA REALM BUDDHIST ASSOCIATION
City of Ten Thousand Buddhas
4951 Bodhi Way, Ukiah
CA 95482 U.S.A.
Tel: (707) 462-0939 Fax: (707) 462-0949
Home Page: http://www.drba.org

Institute for World Religions
(Berkeley Buddhist Monastery)
2304 McKinley Avenue, Berkeley, CA 94703
Tel: (510) 848-3440 Fax: (510) 548-4551

The Administration Women's Headquarters
1825 Magnolia Avenue, Burlingame, CA 94010
Tel/Fax: (650) 692-9286

International Translation Institute
1777 Murchison Drive,
San Francisco, CA 94010
Tel: (650) 692-5912 Fax: (650) 692-5056

The City of the Dharma Realm
1029 West Capitol Ave.,
West Sacramento, CA 95691
Tel/Fax: (916) 374-8268

Gold Mountain Monastery
800 Sacramento Street,
San Francisco, CA 94108
Tel: (415) 421-6117 Fax: (415) 788-6001

Gold Sage Monastery
11455 Clayton Road, San Jose, CA 95127
Tel: (408) 923-7243   Fax: (408) 923-1064

Gold Summit Monastery
233 1st Avenue W., Seattle, WA 98119
Tel: (206) 286-6690   Fax: (206) 284-6918

Gold Wheel Monastery
235 N. Avenue 58, Los Angeles, CA 90042
Tel/Fax: (323) 258-6888

Gold Buddha Monastery
248 E. 11th Avenue, Vancouver
B.C., V5T 2C3 Canada
Tel: (604) 709-0248   Fax: (604) 684-3754

Long Beach Monastery
3361 East Ocean Boulevard,
Long Beach, CA 90803
Tel/Fax: (562) 438-8902

Blessings, Prosperity, & Longevity Monastery
4140 Long Beach Boulevard,
Long Beach, CA 90807
Tel/Fax: (562) 595-4966

Avatamsaka Hermitage
11721 Beally Mountain Road, Potomac,
MD 20854-1128
Tel/Fax: (301) 299-3693

Avatamsaka Monastery
1009 4th Ave. S.W. Calgary,
AB T2P 0K8 Canada
Tel: (403) 234-0644

Dharma Realm Buddhist Books Dist. Society
11th Flr, 85 Chung-hsiao E.Road, Sec. 6,
Taipei, Taiwan, R.O.C.
Tel: (02) 2786-3022; 2786-2474   Fax: (02) 2786-2674

Prajna Guanyin Sagely Monastery
51/2 Miles, Sungai Besi Road,
Salak South, 57100, Kuala Lumpur, Malaysia
Tel: (03) 7982-6560 Fax: (03) 7980-1272

Deng Pi Ang
161, Ampang Road, 50450,
Kuala Lumpur, Malaysia
Tel: (03) 2164-8055 Fax: (03) 2163-7118

Lotus Vihara
136, Jalan Sekolah,
Batang Berjuntai, 45600
Selangor Darul Ehsan, Malaysia
Tel: (03) 3271-9439

Buddhist Lecture Hall
31 Wong Nei Chong Road,
Top Floor, Happy Valley, Hong Kong
Tel: (2) 2572-7644 Fax: (2) 2572-2850